SAFEGUARDING ADULTS

FOCUS ON SOCIAL WORK LAW
Series Editor: Alison Brammer

Palgrave Macmillan's Focus on Social Work Law series consists of compact, accessible guides to the principles, structures and processes of particular areas of the law as they apply to social work practice. Designed to develop students' understanding as well as refresh practitioners' knowledge, each book provides focused, digestible and navigable content in an easily portable form.

Available now

Looked After Children, Caroline Ball
Child Protection, Kim Holt
Capacity and Autonomy, Robert Johns
Making Good Decisions, Michael Preston-Shoot
Children in Need of Support, Joanne Westwood
Safeguarding Adults, Alison Brammer

Forthcoming titles

Court and Legal Skills, Penny Cooper
Adoption and Permanency, Philip Musson
Youth Justice, Jo Staines

Author of the bestselling textbook *Social Work Law*, Alison Brammer is a qualified solicitor with specialist experience working in Social Services, including child protection, adoption, mental health and community care. Alison coordinates the MA in Child Care Law and Practice and the MA in Adult Safeguarding at Keele University.

Series Standing Order

ISBN 9781137017833 paperback
(*outside North America only*)

You can receive future titles in this series as they are published by placing a standing order. Please contact your bookseller or, in the case of difficulty, write to us at the address below with your name and address, the title of the series and the ISBN quoted above.
Customer Services Department, Macmillan Distribution Ltd
Houndmills, Basingstoke, Hampshire RG21 6XS, England

SAFEGUARDING ADULTS

ALISON BRAMMER

palgrave
macmillan

No portion of this publication may be reproduced, copied or transmitted
save with written permission or in accordance with the provisions of the
Copyright, Designs and Patents Act 1988, or under the terms of any licence
permitting limited copying issued by the Copyright Licensing Agency,
Saffron House, 6–10 Kirby Street, London EC1N 8TS.

Any person who does any unauthorized act in relation to this publication
may be liable to criminal prosecution and civil claims for damages.

The author has asserted her right to be identified as the author of this
work in accordance with the Copyright, Designs and Patents Act 1988.

First published 2014 by
PALGRAVE MACMILLAN

Palgrave Macmillan in the UK is an imprint of Macmillan Publishers
Limited, registered in England, company number 785998, of
4 Crinan Street, London N1 9XW.

Palgrave® and Macmillan® are registered trademarks in the United States,
the United Kingdom, Europe and other countries

ISBN: 978–1–137–28995–7

This book is printed on paper suitable for recycling and made from fully
managed and sustained forest sources. Logging, pulping and manufacturing
processes are expected to conform to the environmental regulations of
the country of origin.

A catalogue record for this book is available from the British Library.

A catalog record for this book is available from the Library of Congress.

Typeset by Cambrian Typesetters, Camberley, Surrey

Printed and bound by CPI Group (UK) Ltd, Croydon, CR0 4YY

In memory of Margaret, Barbara and Peter.

CONTENTS

TABLE OF CASES

TABLE OF LEGISLATION AND STATUTORY INSTRUMENTS

ACKNOWLEDGMENTS

I am grateful to all at Palgrave Macmillan for their support, efficiency and patience. Thanks in particular are due to Catherine Gray for her initial invitation to me to be Series Editor and to Lloyd Langman and Helen Caunce for their editorial guidance and encouragement. I am indebted to students on the MA in Adult Safeguarding: Law, Policy and Practice at Keele University whose good humour, professionalism and dedication in this challenging area of practice is an inspiration.

ABBREVIATIONS

ADASS	Association of Directors of Adult Social Services
ADSS	Association of Directors of Social Services
ASW	approved social worker
BASW	British Association of Social Workers
BBC	British Broadcasting Corporation
CPS	Crown Prosecution Service
CQC	Care Quality Commission
CSCI	Commission for Social Care Inspection
DCA	Department for Constitutional Affairs
DBS	Disclosure and Barring Service
DCSF	Department for Children, Schools and Families
DH	Department of Health
DOLS	Deprivation of Liberty Safeguards
ECHR	European Convention on Human Rights 1950
EHRC	Equality and Human Rights Commission
FMU	Forced Marriage Unit
GSCC	General Social Care Council
HCPC	Health and Care Professions Council
HSCIC	Health and Social Care Information Centre
IMCA	Independent Mental Capacity Advocate
IPCC	Independent Police Complaints Commission
LGA	Local Government Association
LGO	Local Government Ombudsman
LPA	lasting power of attorney
MCA 2005	Mental Capacity Act 2005
MoJ	Ministry of Justice
NHS	National Health Service
NHSCCA 1990	National Health Service and Community Care Act 1990
NPIA	National Policing Improvement Agency

OPG	Office of the Public Guardian
POVA	Protection of Vulnerable Adults
PCAW	Public Concern at Work
RAS	Resource Allocation System
RPR	relevant person's representative
SAB	Safeguarding Adults Board
SAR	safeguarding adults review
SCIE	Social Care Institute for Excellence
SVGA 2006	Safeguarding Vulnerable Groups Act 2006

USING THIS BOOK

Aim of the series

Welcome to the Focus on Social Work Law Series.

This introductory section aims to elucidate the aims and philosophy of the series; introduce some key themes that run through the series; outline the key features within each volume; and offer a brief legal skills guide to complement use of the series.

The Social Work Law Focus Series provides a distinct range of specialist resources for students and practitioners. Each volume provides an accessible and practical discussion of the law applicable to a particular area of practice. The length of each volume ensures that whilst portable and focused there is nevertheless a depth of coverage of each topic beyond that typically contained in comprehensive textbooks addressing all aspects of social work law and practice.

Each volume includes the relevant principles, structures and processes of the law (with case law integrated into the text) and highlights clearly the application of the law to practice. A key objective for each text is to identify the policy context of each area of practice and the factors that have shaped the law into its current presentation. As law is constantly developing and evolving, where known, likely future reform of the law is identified. Each book takes a critical approach, noting inconsistencies, omissions and other challenges faced by those charged with its implementation.

The significance of the Human Rights Act 1998 to social work practice is a common theme in each text and implications of the Act for practice in the particular area are identified with inclusion of relevant case law.

The series focuses on the law in England and Wales. Some references may be made to comparable aspects of law in Scotland and Northern Ireland, particularly to highlight differences in approach. With devolution in Scotland and the expanding role of the Welsh Assembly Government it will be important for practitioners in those areas and working at the borders to be familiar with any such differences.

Features

At a glance content lists

Each chapter begins with a bullet point list summarizing the key points within the topic included in that chapter. From this list the reader can see 'at a glance' how the materials are organized and what to expect in that section. The introductory chapter provides an overview of the book, outlining coverage in each chapter that enables the reader to see how the topic develops throughout the text. The boundaries of the discussion are set including, where relevant, explicit recognition of areas that are excluded from the text.

Key case analysis

One of the key aims of the series is to emphasize an integrated under-standing of law, comprising legislation and case law and practice. For this reason each chapter includes at least one key case analysis feature focusing on a particularly significant case. The facts of the case are outlined in brief followed by analysis of the implications of the deci-sion for social work practice in a short commentary. Given the signifi-cance of the selected cases, readers are encouraged to follow up references and read the case in full together with any published commentaries.

On-the-spot questions

These questions are designed to consolidate learning and prompt reflection on the material considered. These questions may be used as a basis for discussion with colleagues or fellow students and may also prompt consideration or further investigation of how the law is applied within a particular setting or authority, for example, looking at informa-tion provided to service users on a council website. Questions may also follow key cases, discussion of research findings or practice scenarios, focusing on the issues raised and application of the relevant law to practice.

Practice focus

Each volume incorporates practice-focused case scenarios to demon-strate how the law is applied to social work practice. The scenarios may be fictional or based on an actual decision.

Further reading

Each chapter closes with suggestions for further reading to develop knowledge and critical understanding. Annotated to explain the reasons for inclusion, the reader may be directed to classic influential pieces, such as enquiry reports, up-to-date research and analysis of issues discussed in the chapter, and relevant policy documents. In addition students may wish to read in full the case law included throughout the text and to follow up references integrated into discussion of each topic.

Websites

As further important sources of information, websites are also included in the text with links from the companion website. Some may be a gateway to access significant documents including government publications, others may provide accessible information for service users or present a particular perspective on an area, such as the voices of experts by experience. Given the rapid development of law and practice across the range of topics covered in the series, reference to relevant websites can be a useful way to keep pace with actual and anticipated changes.

Glossary

Each text includes a subject-specific glossary of key terms for quick reference and clarification. A flashcard version of the glossary is available on the companion website.

Visual aids

As appropriate, visual aids are included where information may be presented accessibly as a table, graph or flow chart. This approach is particularly helpful for the presentation of some complex areas of law and to demonstrate structured decision-making or options available.

Companion site

The series-wide companion site www.palgrave.com/socialworklaw provides additional learning resources, including flashcard glossaries, web links, a legal skills guide, and a blog to communicate important developments and updates. The site will also host a student feedback zone.

Key sources of law

In this section an outline of the key sources of law considered through-out the series is provided. The following 'Legal skills' section includes some guidance on the easiest ways to access and understand these sources.

Legislation

The term legislation is used interchangeably with Acts of Parliament and statutes to refer to primary sources of law.

All primary legislation is produced through the parliamentary process, beginning its passage as a Bill. Bills may have their origins as an expressed policy in a government manifesto, in the work of the Law Commission, or following and responding to a significant event such as a child death or the work of a government department such as the Home Office.

Each Bill is considered by both the House of Lords and House of Commons, debated and scrutinized through various committee stages before becoming an Act on receipt of royal assent.

Legislation has a title and year, for example, the Equality Act 2010. Legislation can vary in length from an Act with just one section to others with over a hundred. Lengthy Acts are usually divided into headed 'Parts' (like chapters) containing sections, subsections and paragraphs. For example, s. 31 of the Children Act 1989 is in Part IV entitled 'Care and Supervision' and outlines the criteria for care order applications. Beyond the main body of the Act the legislation may also include 'Schedules' following the main provisions. Schedules have the same force of law as the rest of the Act but are typically used to cover detail such as a list of legislation which has been amended or revoked by the current Act or detailed matters linked to a specific provision, for instance, Schedule 2 of the Children Act 1989 details specific services (e.g. day centres) which may be provided under the duty to safeguard and promote the welfare of children in need, contained in s. 17.

Remember also that statutes often contain sections dealing with inter-pretation or definitions and, although often situated towards the end of the Act, these can be a useful starting point.

Legislation also includes Statutory Instruments which may be in the form of rules, regulations and orders. The term delegated legislation collectively describes this body of law as it is made under delegated authority of Parliament, usually by a minister or government department. Statutory Instruments tend to provide additional detail to the outline scheme provided by the primary legislation, the Act of Parliament. Statutory Instruments are usually cited by year and a number, for example, Local Authority Social Services (Complaints Procedure) Order SI 2006/1681.

Various documents may be issued to further assist with the implementation of legislation including guidance and codes of practice.

Guidance

Guidance documents may be described as formal or practice guidance. Formal guidance may be identified as such where it is stated to have been issued under s. 7(1) of the Local Authority Social Services Act 1970, which provides that 'local authorities shall act under the general guidance of the Secretary of State'. An example of s. 7 guidance is *Working Together to Safeguard Children* (2013, London: Department of Health). The significance of s. 7 guidance was explained by Sedley J in *R v London Borough of Islington, ex parte Rixon* [1997] ELR 66: 'Parliament in enacting s. 7(1) did not intend local authorities to whom ministerial guidance was given to be free, having considered it, to take it or leave it … in my view parliament by s. 7(1) has required local authorities to follow the path charted by the Secretary of State's guidance, with liberty to deviate from it where the local authority judges on admissible grounds that there is good reason to do so, but without freedom to take a substantially different course.' (71)

Practice guidance does not carry s. 7 status but should nevertheless normally be followed as setting examples of what good practice might look like.

Codes of practice

Codes of practice have been issued to support the Mental Health Act 1983 and the Mental Capacity Act 2005. Again, it is a matter of good practice to follow the recommendations of the codes and these lengthy documents include detailed and illustrative scenarios to assist with interpretation and application of the legislation. There may also be a duty on specific people charged with responsibilities under the primary legislation to have regard to the code.

Guidance and codes of practice are available on relevant websites, for example, the Department of Health, as referenced in individual volumes.

Case law

Case law provides a further major source of law. In determining disputes in court the judiciary applies legislation. Where provisions within legislation are unclear or ambiguous the judiciary follows principles of statutory interpretation but at times judges are quite creative.

Some areas of law are exclusively contained in case law and described as common law. Most law of relevance to social work practice is of relatively recent origin and has its primary basis in legislation. Case law remains relevant as it links directly to such legislation and may clarify and explain provisions and terminology within the legislation. The significance of a particular decision will depend on the position of the court in a hierarchy whereby the Supreme Court is most senior and the Magistrates' Court is junior. Decisions of the higher courts bind the lower courts – they must be followed. This principle is known as the doctrine of precedent. Much legal debate takes place as to the precise element of a ruling which subsequently binds other decisions. This is especially the case where in the Court of Appeal or Supreme Court there are between three and five judges hearing a case, majority judgments are allowed and different judges may arrive at the same conclusion but for different reasons. Where a judge does not agree with the majority, the term dissenting judgment is applied.

It is important to understand how cases reach court. Many cases in social work law are based on challenges to the way a local authority has exercised its powers. This is an aspect of administrative law known as judicial review where the central issue for the court is not the substance of the decision taken by the authority but the way it was taken. Important considerations will be whether the authority has exceeded its powers, failed to follow established procedures or acted irrationally.

Before an individual can challenge an authority in judicial review it will usually be necessary to exhaust other remedies first, including local authority complaints procedures. If unsatisfied with the outcome of a complaint an individual has a further option which is to complain to the Local Government Ombudsman (LGO). The LGO investigates alleged cases of maladministration and may make recommendations to local authorities including the payment of financial compensation. Ombudsman decisions may be accessed on the LGO website and make interesting reading. In cases involving social services, a common concern across children's and adults' services is unreasonable delay in carrying out assessments and providing services. See www.lgo.org.uk.

Classification of law

The above discussion related to the sources and status of laws. It is also important to note that law can serve a variety of functions and may be grouped into recognized classifications. For law relating to social work practice key classifications distinguish between law which is criminal or civil and law which is public or private.

Whilst acknowledging the importance of these classifications, it must also be appreciated that individual concerns and circumstances may not always fall so neatly into the same categories, a given scenario may engage with criminal, civil, public and private law.

- Criminal law relates to alleged behaviour which is defined by statute or common law as an offence prosecuted by the state, carrying a penalty which may include imprisonment. The offence must be proved 'beyond reasonable doubt'.
- Civil law is the term applied to all other areas of law and often focuses on disputes between individuals. A lower standard of proof, 'balance of probabilities', applies in civil cases.
- Public law is that in which society has some interest and involves a public authority, such as care proceedings.
- Private law operates between individuals, such as marriage or contract.

Legal skills guide: accessing and understanding the law

Legislation

Legislation may be accessed as printed copies published by The Stationery Office and is also available online. Some books on a particular area of law will include a copy of the Act (sometimes anno-tated) and this is a useful way of learning about new laws. As time goes by, however, and amendments are made to legislation it can become increasingly difficult to keep track of the up-to-date version of an Act. Revised and up-to-date versions of legislation (as well as the version originally enacted) are available on the website www.legislation.gov.uk.

Legislation may also be accessed on the Parliament website. Here, it is possible to trace the progress of current and draft Bills and a link to Hansard provides transcripts of debates on Bills as they pass through both Houses of Parliament, www.parliament.uk.

Bills and new legislation are often accompanied by 'Explanatory notes' which can give some background to the development of the new law and offer useful explanations of each provision.

Case law

Important cases are reported in law reports available in traditional bound volumes (according to court, specialist area or general weekly reports) or online. Case referencing is known as citation and follows particular conventions according to whether a hard copy law report or online version is sought.

Citation of cases in law reports begins with the names of the parties, followed by the year and volume number of the law report, followed by an abbreviation of the law report title, then the page number. For example: *Lawrence v Pembrokeshire CC* [2007] 2 FLR 705. The case is reported in volume 2 of the 2007 Family Law Report at page 705.

Online citation, sometimes referred to as neutral citation because it is not linked to a particular law report, also starts with the names of the parties, followed by the year in which the case was decided, followed by an abbreviation of the court in which the case was heard, followed by a number representing the place in the order of cases decided by that court. For example: *R (Macdonald) v Royal Borough of Kensington and Chelsea* [2011] UKSC 33. Neutral citation of this case shows that it was a 2011 decision of the Supreme Court.

University libraries tend to have subscriptions to particular legal databases, such as 'Westlaw', which can be accessed by those enrolled as students, often via direct links from the university library webpage. Westlaw and LexisNexis are especially useful as sources of case law, statutes and other legal materials. Libraries usually have their own guides to these sources, again often published on their websites. For most cases there is a short summary or analysis as well as the full transcript.

As not everyone using the series will be enrolled at a university, the following website can be accessed without any subscription: BAILLI (British and Irish Legal Information Institute) www.bailii.org. This site includes judgments from the full range of UK court services including the Supreme Court, Court of Appeal and High Court but also features a wide range of tribunal decisions. Judgments for Scotland, Northern Ireland and the Republic of Ireland are also available as are judgments of the European Court of Human Rights.

Whether accessed via a law report or online, the presentation of cases follows a template. The report begins with the names of the parties, the court which heard the cases, names(s) of the judges(s) and dates of the hearing. This is followed by a summary of key legal issues involved in the case (often in italics) known as catchwords, then the headnote, which is a paragraph or so stating the key facts of the case and the nature of the claim or dispute or the criminal charge. 'HELD' indicates the ruling of the court. This is followed by a list of cases that were referred to in legal argument during the hearing, a summary of the journey of the case through appeal processes, names of the advocates and then the start of the full judgment(s) given by the judge(s). The judgment usually recounts the circumstances of the case, findings of fact and findings on the law and reasons for the decision.

If stuck on citations the Cardiff Index to Legal Abbreviations is a useful resource at www.legalabbrevs.cardiff.ac.uk.

There are numerous specific guides to legal research providing more detailed examination of legal materials but the best advice on developing legal skills is to start exploring the above and to read some case law – it's surprisingly addictive!

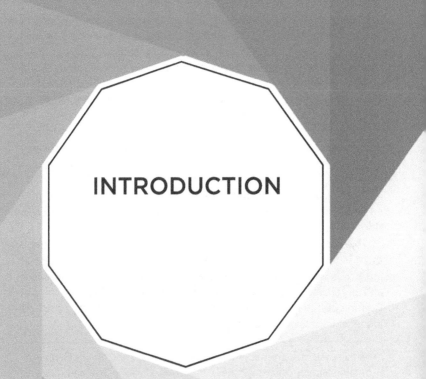

INTRODUCTION

AT A GLANCE THIS CHAPTER COVERS:

- emergence of adult safeguarding as a social problem
- essential terminology
- attempts to arrive at a definition of adult abuse
- types of abuse
- extent of abuse
- subject of abuse
- use of law
- impact of the Human Rights Act 1998
- outline of subsequent chapters

Safeguarding adults has been identified as a key area of social work practice. In terms of recognition and development of practice it is in its infancy compared with, for example, child protection, youth justice or mental health. The aim of this text is to provide a clear and accessible guide to a subject that is not considered in all of the established texts (or in any great detail), and also does not feature as prominently as other areas of practice, notably child protection, on qualifying courses. It is, however, an area which is attracting greater media attention with high-profile cases, such as: the death of Margaret Panting (which resulted in an extension of the crime of causing or allowing the death of a child, to also include vulnerable adults); the death of Steven Hoskin in Cornwall (a man with learning disabilities killed by those who had befriended him), published in a **serious case review**; and the events at Winterbourne View Hospital, as highlighted in the BBC *Panorama* documentary.

The challenge of understanding the relevant law is also greater as there is no single piece of legislation to which to refer and there are numerous practice and ethical dilemmas in balancing risk, autonomy and protection. This complexity has been acknowledged by the **Law Commission** in its review of adult social care law, stating that the existing legal framework for adult protection is:

> neither systematic nor coordinate, reflecting the sporadic development of safeguarding policy over the last 25 years. Unlike in Scotland, there is no single or coherent statutory framework for adult protection in England and Wales. Instead it must be discerned through reference to a wide range of law including general community care legislation and guidance, the Mental Health Act 1983, the Mental Capacity Act 2005, the Safeguarding Vulnerable Groups Act 2006, the **inherent jurisdiction** of the High Court, and the civil and criminal justice systems.
>
> *Law Commission, 2011a: para. 9.1*

This introductory chapter focuses on the emergence of safeguarding adults as an area of practice and the recognition of the abuse of adults. It begins with discussion of definitions, types of abuse and prevalence. The role and use of law is considered and the actual and potential impact of the Human Rights Act 1998 is introduced.

In this chapter and throughout the text an indication of changes to terminology and substance of the law in the light of the Law Commission consultation (2011a) and the Care Act 2014 are included. The text primarily focuses on the law in England with some references to the position in Wales and Scotland by way of comparison.

Defining abuse

Within a text focusing on law relating to safeguarding adults from abuse it is essential to have an understanding of key terminology and definitions. Both definitions of abuse and of the subject of abuse have proven to be a challenge, being problematic conceptually, ethically and legally. Those working in the field need to have an understanding of current formal definitions as they may present a gateway to responses. At the same time it is essential to retain a critical eye, have an awareness of the potential of definitions to discriminate and stigmatize, and acknowledge the necessary fluidity of definitions in an area of developing knowledge and awareness.

The first formal definition appeared in guidance from the Department of Health (DH) with a focus on abuse of older people in their own homes:

> Abuse may be described as physical, sexual, psychological or financial. It may be intentional or the result of neglect. It may cause harm to the older person, either temporarily or over a period of time. (DH and Social Services Inspectorate, 1993)

This was followed by a definition formulated by Action on Elder Abuse, again focusing on older people:

> Elder abuse is a single or repeated act or lack of appropriate action occurring within any relationship where there is an expectation of trust, which causes harm or distress to an older person. (Action on Elder Abuse, 1994)

The key current definition was introduced in *No Secrets: Guidance on Developing and Implementing Multi-agency Policies and Procedures to Protect Vulnerable Adults from Abuse* (DH, 2000b). This is statutory guidance which has recently been the subject of consultation and review but is likely to remain in place until the wider adult social care law reforms are finalized. The guidance is discussed fully in Chapter 1. The definition introduced by *No Secrets* applies to 'vulnerable adults' (discussed below) and hence is a wider remit than the earlier definitions, which focused on older people. It also has a differing conceptual basis, located in a rights discourse and clearly influenced by the timely introduction of the Human

Rights Act 1998. This definition is included in most local authority policies and procedures:

> Abuse is a violation of an individual's human and civil rights by any other person or persons. (DH, 2000b:2.5)

The following paragraph provides further elaboration of the central definition:

> Abuse may consist of a single or repeated acts. It may be physical, verbal, or psychological, it may be an act of neglect or an omission to act, or it may occur when a vulnerable person is persuaded to enter into a financial or sexual transaction to which s/he has not consented, or cannot consent. Abuse can occur in any relationship and may result in significant harm to, or exploitation of, the person.
>
> *DH, 2000b:2.6*

Key categories of abuse are also identified, with some explanation and examples:

> **physical abuse,** including hitting, slapping, pushing, kicking, misuse of medication, restraint, or inappropriate sanctions;
>
> **sexual abuse,** including rape and sexual assault or sexual acts to which the vulnerable adult has not consented, or could not consent or was pressured into consenting;
>
> **psychological abuse,** including emotional abuse, threats of harm or abandonment, deprivation of contact, humiliation, blaming, controlling, intimidation, coercion, harassment, verbal abuse, isolation or withdrawal from services or supportive networks;
>
> **financial or material abuse,** including theft, fraud, exploitation, pressure in connection with wills, property or inheritance or financial transactions, or the misuse or misappropriation of property, possessions or benefits;
>
> **neglect and acts of omission,** including ignoring medical or physical care needs, failure to provide access to appropriate health, social care or educational services, the withholding of the necessities of life, such as medication, adequate nutrition and heating; and
>
> **discriminatory abuse,** including racist, sexist, that based on a person's disability, and other forms of harassment, slurs or similar treatment.
>
> *DH, 2000b:2.7* [original emphasis]

Institutional abuse is mentioned later in *No Secrets* (2.9). The guidance recognizes the complexity and range of abuse scenarios, acknowledging that the context and perpetrator of abuse may be various and that in relation to motivation: 'Any or all of these types of abuse may be perpetrated as the result of deliberate intent, negligence or ignorance.' (2.7) Whilst categorization of different types of abuse is useful, it is important to remember that an individual may suffer from more than one type of abuse. Indeed, it would be unusual for an individual to suffer sexual or physical abuse without an element of psychological abuse. Cambridge et al. (2011) suggest that the most common form of abuse is multiple abuse. Some research has focused on particular types of abuse, for instance, financial abuse (Gilhooly et al., 2013), and levels of awareness and recognition may vary between types of abuse. For example, sexual abuse was described by Action on Elder Abuse as ' the great taboo' (2000; see also Brown et al., 1995; Jeary, 2004).

An alternative conceptualization is provided by Flynn and Brown (2010). They suggest that types of abuse can be classified according to the following features: hate crimes; predatory crimes; parasitic crimes; risks arising out of service settings; breaches of professional boundaries; family violence, neglect or negligence; unethical or unauthorized practice; and discriminatory access to public resources. Herring (2009) prefers to focus on just three key elements of categorization, namely: domestic abuse; institutional abuse; self-neglect or self-abuse.

Most local authority policies and procedures have adopted the *No Secrets* categories and this continues to offer a useful starting point. Since 2000, however, knowledge and awareness of abuse and possible further categories of abuse have grown and it is essential to be receptive to 'new' categories. Recognition of forms of child abuse has experienced the same growth, with recently recognized forms being, for example, cyber-bullying, impact of witnessing domestic violence and fabricated illness. A revised version of *No Secrets* is likely to take account of the developing nature of abuse. In addition, the formulation in new legislation appears to allow scope for interpretation.

There are broader questions about the extent of safeguarding practice and the necessity to balance concepts of autonomy and protection. Some caution might be necessary in casting a wide net for potential intervention. Additional categories to have emerged since *No Secrets* and which might need to be encompassed within safeguarding practice could include: self-neglect; self-harm; hate crime; domestic abuse; forced marriage; trafficking; and overuse of medication. Research recently commissioned by the DH (Braye et al., 2011a) described the concept of self-neglect as complex and found that, despite its omission from a formal definition, 'safeguarding structures and communication channels are commonly used to facilitate information sharing about situations of self-neglect, and to resolve questions of whether intervention can be made' (Braye et al., 2011a). The same study notes that in the USA self-neglect comprises the greater proportion of cases facing adult protection services. In the UK self-neglect has featured in a number of serious case reviews, e.g. Sheffield Adult Safeguarding Partnership Board, *Serious Case Review: Ann* (Flynn, 2010), and it seems that there is a need for consistency in approach to self-neglect cases.

Hate crimes appear to have featured in some of the reported serious case reviews following the death or harm of a vulnerable adult and such cases are not always conceptualized as safeguarding matters. For example, in the case of Fiona Pilkington and her daughter no **referral** was ever made to safeguarding. The Equality and Human Rights Commission (EHRC), in its analysis of a number of serious case reviews also noted this disconnect, stating:

> The cases of disability-related harassment which come to court and receive media attention are only the tip of the iceberg: there is a systemic failure by public authorities to recognize the extent and impact of harassment and abuse of disabled people, take action to prevent it happening in the first place and intervene effectively when it does ... there was a failure to share intelligence and coordinate responses across different services and organizations.
>
> *EHRC, 2011b:3*

The Care Act 2014 will provide a new framework for adult social care law and includes some safeguarding provisions. The new proposals are discussed throughout the text alongside the relevant existing law. In addition to new legislation, once the Bill receives royal assent, there are likely to be further rules and regulations, guidance and possibly a Code of Practice supplying additional details and guidance. As it stands, s. 42(3) Care Act 2014 provides the following definition of abuse:

s. 42

(3) 'Abuse' includes financial abuse; and for that purpose 'financial abuse' includes—

(a) having money or other property stolen,

(b) being defrauded,

(c) being put under pressure in relation to money or other property, and

(d) having money or other property misused.

Care Act 2014

Neglect is not defined. The emphasis on financial abuse and lack of direct reference to other types of abuse presents a somewhat distorted view, however, elaboration in guidance might be expected.

On-the-spot questions	1 Is it necessary to classify different types of abuse? 2 Why?

Prevalence

The results of a national prevalence study into the abuse and neglect of older people in domestic settings were published in 2007 (O'Keefe et al., 2007). The study comprised a survey of 2100 people throughout the UK, aged 66 and over in private households (i.e. people in residential and nursing accommodation were not included). Utilizing the term 'mistreatment' to include abuse and neglect, the survey found that 4 per cent of people had experienced mistreatment involving a family member, close friend, care worker, neighbour or acquaintance. In this survey, neglect was the most common form of mistreatment, followed by financial abuse. The full report provides a breakdown by country, age and sex (and other categories), considers the characteristics of perpetrators and the impact of mistreatment, and concludes that its estimate is likely to be conservative.

Records of referrals to safeguarding teams provide an additional source of data. The Health and Social Care Information Centre (HSCIC) (2013) published 'experimental statistics' covering the period 1 April 2012 to 31 March 2013, drawn from returns from the 152 councils with adult social services responsibilities. Data is included as to: who is being abused; what type of abuse is happening (following the *No Secrets* classification and therefore excluding self-neglect); where abuse is taking place; and the relationship between alleged victim and perpetrator. Key findings included that over the year there were 176,000

alerts about safeguarding (not all councils recorded the initial alert stage and this information is based on the returns of 119 councils). The total number of referrals from 152 councils, i.e. those cases which met local safeguarding thresholds, reached 109,000, of which 43 per cent were wholly or partly substantiated. Analysis of the detail of those referrals found that 61 per cent of referrals were for women and 62 per cent were for adults aged over 65. Referrals were more likely to be made by health and social care staff (66 per cent) than family members (11 per cent). The breakdown into categories of abuse identified allegations of physical abuse at 28 per cent, neglect at 27 per cent, financial abuse at 18 per cent, emotional or psychological abuse at 16 per cent, sexual abuse at 5 per cent, institutional abuse at 4 per cent and discriminatory abuse at 1 per cent. The most likely setting for abuse was the person's own home (39 per cent of cases), followed by cases in care homes (36 per cent). Perpetrators were recorded in cases as family members (23 per cent), social care staff (32 per cent), other vulnerable adults (12 per cent), friends, neighbours, volunteers, other professionals or strangers (10 per cent), health care workers (5 per cent) and other or unknown (19 per cent). Outcomes data is also included in this report and ranged from no further action (29 per cent), increased monitoring (28 per cent) and other (12 per cent), to community care assessment and services (10 per cent). Predictably, there are some limitations to the statistics. It is unclear, for example, why the classification of perpetrators would group strangers with friends and other professionals. Not all councils were able to submit a complete return, which suggests inconsistency in data collection. Nevertheless, there is a level of detail in this report which gives a real indication of safeguarding activity in England.

Prevalence studies have been carried out throughout the world and, unsurprisingly, prevalence rates vary because different definitions and methods are utilized. A systematic review conducted by Cooper et al. (2008) focused on studies of elder abuse and neglect and found that one in four older people were at risk of abuse and only a small proportion of this came to the attention of protective services. Other sources of anecdotal evidence include helpline accounts and reports of the first-tier tribunal where the Care Quality Commission (CQC) has intervened to provide accounts of abuse in residential settings.

On-the-spot
questions

1 Why is it important to measure the extent of abuse?
2 What difficulties are likely to arise in any attempt to measure the extent of abuse?

The subject of abuse

The term 'vulnerable adult' is used throughout *No Secrets*. A vulnerable adult is a person over 18:

> who is or may be in need of community care services by reason of mental or other disability, age or illness;
> and who is or may be unable to take care of him or herself, or unable to protect him or herself against significant harm or exploitation (DH, 2000b:2.3).

'Vulnerable adult' has become a contentious term and, increasingly, it is being replaced by the term 'adult at risk' as features in the Adult Support and Protection (Scotland) Act 2007. The Association of Directors of Social Services (ADSS) (2005) noted that vulnerability can be misunderstood, because it seems to locate the cause of the abuse with the victim, rather than placing responsibility with the actions or omissions of others. More recently, the Law Commission (2012) described the term as 'stigmatising, dated, negative and disempowering'.

The term does not directly feature in the Care Act 2014, which instead refers to an adult who:

s. 40

(a) Has needs for care and support (whether or not the authority is meeting any of those needs),
(b) Is experiencing, or is at risk of, abuse or neglect, and
(c) As a result of those needs is unable to protect him/herself against the abuse or neglect or the risk of it.

Care Act 2014

Whilst new guidance and legislation may not include reference to the vulnerable adult, it is a term which will endure as it exists elsewhere and is defined variously in, for example, the Care Standards Act 2000, the Domestic Violence, Crime and Victims Act 2004 and the Youth Justice and Criminal Evidence Act 1999. In addition a line of case law has developed in which the **powers** of the inherent jurisdiction have been exercised in relation to the need to safeguard a particular 'vulnerable adult', for which the term, 'Munby vulnerable' has been loosely coined.

The term originated in the case *Re SA (Vulnerable Adult with Capacity: Marriage)* [2005]. The case concerned an 18-year-old woman who was profoundly deaf and partially sighted and whose only means of communication was British Sign Language which her Punjabi-speaking family did not use. The court had to consider whether it could continue the protection offered in her minority to protect her from the risk of an unsuitable arranged marriage. It was accepted that she did not lack the capacity to marry and understood the concept of marriage, but would have difficulty understanding a specific marriage contract to a specific individual which would involve moving to Pakistan.

Lord Justice Munby stated:

> the inherent jurisdiction can be exercised in relation to a vulnerable adult who, even if not incapacitated ... is, or is reasonably believed to be, either (i) under constraint or (ii) subject to coercion or undue influence or (iii) for some other reason deprived of the capacity to make the relevant decision, or disabled from making a free choice, or incapacitated or disabled from giving a real and genuine consent. [77] ...
>
> I would treat as a vulnerable adult someone who, whether or not mentally incapacitated, and whether or not suffering from any mental illness or mental disorder, is or may be unable to take care of himself, or unable to protect himself against significant harm or exploitation, or who is deaf, blind or dumb, or substantially handicapped by illness, injury or congenital deformity. This, is not and is not intended to be a definition. It is descriptive, not definitive; indicative rather than prescriptive. [82]
>
> Re SA (Vulnerable Adult with Capacity: Marriage) *[2005]*

Prior to the introduction of the Mental Capacity Act 2005 (MCA 2005) the inherent jurisdiction was utilized in relation to adults who lacked capacity in relation to a particular matter, such as medical treatment (*Re MB (Caesarean Section)* [1997]), contact (*Re D-R (Adult: Contact)* [1999]) and country of residence (*Re S (Hospital Patient: Court's Jurisdiction)* [1996]). In the significant case of *Re F (Adult: Court's Jurisdiction)* [2000], the local authority had safeguarding concerns for a young woman who lacked capacity, who could not be protected by either the provisions of the Children Act 1989, wardship or the Mental Health Act 1983. The court made orders stipulating that she should reside in local authority accommodation and defining the contact she should have with her mother.

Since the introduction of the MCA 2005, the **Court of Protection** has assumed that jurisdiction and can make **declarations** in respect of adults who lack capacity in accordance with the capacity test in s. 2 of the legislation. The vulnerable adult as defined by Munby is broader than the definition of an adult who lacks capacity for the purposes of the MCA 2005 and also potentially broader than the *No Secrets* definition as there is no required link to eligibility for community care services. The continued existence of the inherent jurisdiction for adults who may have capacity under the MCA 2005 but are nevertheless considered vulnerable has been confirmed by the Court of Appeal in *DL v A Local Authority and Others* [2012], an important case for safeguarding adults practice.

> → KEY CASE ANALYSIS ←

DL v A Local Authority and Others [2012]

The facts of the case are set out in the judgment of the court as follows:

> The case concerns an elderly married couple, Mr and Mrs L who live with their son DL who is in his fifties. Mrs L is disabled and receives direct payments and community care support. At the time the proceedings were commenced it was accepted that Mr and Mrs L had capacity to manage their affairs and decide whether their son should live with them and what their relationship would be. By the time the matter came before Theis J in the High Court Mr L had moved into a care home and was assessed not to have capacity to make his own decisions. Concerns over the son's alleged aggressive behaviour towards his parents prompted the local authority application to obtain protection for them from him. It is clear that the local authority had been involved with the family for some time.
>
> The local authority has documented incidents going back to 2005 which, it says, chronicle DL's behaviour and which include physical assaults, verbal threats, controlling where and when his parents may move in the house, preventing them from leaving the house, and controlling who may visit them, and the terms upon which they may visit them, including

> health and social care professionals providing care and support for Mrs L. There have also been consistent reports that DL is seeking to coerce Mr L into transferring the ownership of the house into DL's name and that he has also placed considerable pressure on both his parents to have Mrs L moved into a care home against her wishes. [6]

An independent social work expert produced a written report for the full hearing in which he concluded that GRL and ML had capacity to decide on residence and contact for the purposes of the MCA 2005, however, he considered that 'both GRL and ML are unduly influenced by DL to an extent that their capacity (in the SA sense) to make balanced and considered decisions is compromised or prevented' [6].

LJ McFarlane captured the point of law at stake:

> the focus of this appeal is a single point of law ... the extent to which the inherent jurisdiction of the High Court may be deployed following the implementation of the MCA 2005 for the protection of adults who are perceived to be vulnerable ... whether a jurisdictional hinterland exists outside its borders to deal with cases of 'vulnerable adults' who fall outside that Act. [1]

He confirmed the continued availability of the inherent jurisdiction as an important 'safety net'.

In a criminal law context reference will be made to victims and perpetrators. Whether referring to crime or abuse it is simplistic to assume that it is always possible to clearly differentiate between a perpetrator and a victim and these roles may blur (McKeough and Knell-Taylor, 2002).

Use of law

In many areas of social care the decision about when and how to invoke the law is complex. This is particularly so in relation to safeguarding adults in the absence of a clear statutory framework with a discernible objective supported by principles to guide its application. Nevertheless, it is clear from *No Secrets* that there is a role for the law:

> Action might be primarily supportive or therapeutic or it might involve the application of sanctions, suspension, regulatory activity or criminal prosecution, disciplinary action

or de-registration from a professional body. Remember, vulnerable adults who are victims, like any other victims, have a right to see justice. (DH, 2000b:6.4)

The scope of legal intervention envisaged by *No Secrets* has a range of purposes. In their discussion of the role of law, Parker and Penhale (2007) suggest three separate purposes for the law: preventative, ameliorative/remedial and punitive. The punitive approach has its foundations in the operation of the criminal law, and again this approach is envisaged by *No Secrets*:

> Some instances of abuse will constitute a criminal offence. In this respect vulnerable adults are entitled to the protection of law in the same way as any other member of the public ... Examples of actions which may constitute criminal offences are assault, whether physical or psychological, sexual assault and rape, theft, fraud or other forms of financial exploitation, and certain forms of discrimination, whether on racial or gender grounds ... Criminal investigation by the police takes priority over all other lines of enquiry.
>
> *DH, 2000b:2.8*

No Secrets includes principles to guide good practice, one of which is to 'ensure that the law and statutory requirements are known and used appropriately so that vulnerable adults receive the protection of the law'. Knowing the law is an exacting requirement given the speed and volume of legal developments over recent years. Below is a list of the statutes enacted since *No Secrets* with relevance to safeguarding practice to which the range of supplementary guidance, codes of practice and case law must be added:

- Care Standards Act 2000;
- Carers and Disabled Children Act 2000;
- Freedom of Information Act 2000;
- Race Relations (Amendment) Act 2000;
- Sexual Offences Act 2003;
- Carers (Equal Opportunities) Act 2004;
- Civil Partnership Act 2004;
- Domestic Violence Crime and Victims Act 2004;
- Gender Recognition Act 2004;
- Disability Discrimination Act 2005;

- Mental Capacity Act 2005;
- Safeguarding Vulnerable Groups Act 2006;
- Mental Health Act 2007;
- Forced Marriage (Civil Protection) Act 2007;
- Health and Social Care Act 2008;
- Equality Act 2010;
- Health and Social Care Act 2012; and
- Care Act 2014.

The key is to find ways of navigating the mass of law. Models may include classification of relevant law according to the type of abuse or by the objective sought in utilizing law (Brammer, 2001). In any consideration of the use of law in safeguarding it is appropriate to commit to the principle of least intervention necessary to achieve a positive outcome and essential to act compatibly with the Human Rights Act 1998 and to comply with professional standards. The recent advice note to Directors of Adult Social Services reinforces the above discussion, noting:

> There is a range of criminal, civil and other powers and duties to support the practice of adult safeguarding, however , we have found that **many of these are underused** and that practitioners are not as aware of them as they ought to be. Directors should therefore make sure your staff are **legally literate,** that is they know what these powers are and when and how to use them in the best interest of the person at risk of harm. They should also be sufficiently trained, up to date and have easy access to legal advice when they need it.
>
> *Association of Directors of Adult Social Services (ADASS) and Local Government Association (LGA), 2013:16* [original emphasis]

Application of the Human Rights Act 1998

Cases which have involved human rights arguments will be incorporated throughout the text. At this stage it is appropriate to identify the key Articles from the European Convention on Human Rights (ECHR) and their potential application to safeguarding adults.

The table opposite provides a simplified version of the Articles with brief illustrations of possible areas of engagement with safeguarding. Application of the Convention is considered further throughout the text, including relevant case law.

Article	Right, prohibition or restriction	Application to safeguarding
Article 2	Right to life	Euthanasia, age-related treatment decisions, prevention of suicide
Article 3	Prohibition against torture or inhuman or degrading treatment or punishment	Abuse Positive obligation on local authority to protect individuals
Article 4	Prohibition against slavery or servitude, forced or compulsory labour	Trafficking
Article 5	Right to liberty and security of person	**Deprivation of Liberty Safeguards** (DOLS)
Article 6	Right to a fair and public hearing within a reasonable time by an independent and impartial tribunal	Complaints procedures, disclosure of information, **special measures**
Article 8	Right to respect for private and family life, home and correspondence	Integrity of the person, provision of support, contact Any interference must be proportionate
Article 9	Right to freedom of thought, conscience and religion; freedom to manifest religion or belief	Respect for different religious ceremonies, practices and dress within services
Article 10	Right to freedom of expression … to receive and impart information	Whistleblowing Publication of information in appropriate formats
Article 12	Right to marry and to found a family	Non-therapeutic sterilizations Test for capacity to marry
Article 14	Enjoyment of rights and freedoms … shall be secured without discrimination on any grounds such as sex, race, colour, language, religion, political or other opinion, national or social origin, association with a national minority, property, birth or other status	'Other status' could apply to age Discrimination against 'vulnerable adults' in the enjoyment of the above Articles

Table 1.1: Key Articles from the ECHR

Cases may concern violation of a single Article but multiple breaches may occur, as in the following case.

> ➔ **KEY CASE ANALYSIS** ⬅
>
> *ZH v Commissioner of Police for the Metropolis* [2013]
>
> A 16-year-old boy with severe autism and epilepsy was taken swimming and refused to move from the poolside. His carers were unable to move him with distraction techniques. Police attended and were informed of his autism. When one of them touched the boy he jumped into the pool. He was lifted, struggling, out of the pool and the police restrained him with handcuffs and leg restraints. He was then placed in a cage in the police van.
>
> It was found that the police had inflicted inhuman or degrading treatment on the boy considering the duration of force and restraint, injuries to the boy and his age, health and vulnerability. He was deprived of his liberty as the nature and duration of the restraint amounted to more than a restriction on movement. The police actions also interfered with the boy's right to respect for his private life and could not be justified as proportionate as less intrusive action could have been taken. Human rights claims under Articles 3, 5 and 8 were successful. Damages were awarded. The court noted that: 'The case highlights the need for there to be an awareness of the disability of autism within the public services.' The appeal by the police against the award of damages was dismissed by the Court of Appeal, where judgment was particularly critical of the failure of the police to consult properly with the care workers.

From this broad introduction subsequent chapters focus on particular aspects of the law as outlined below.

Outline of chapters

Chapter 1: guidance, policies and procedures

No Secrets (DH, 2000b) has been subject to a consultation review but remains the key guidance for local authorities as lead responsibility for safeguarding. This chapter will discuss the status of *No Secrets*, outline its key features, including the expected procedure for safeguarding cases, as well as recognizing its limitations, in particular the absence of a statutory **duty** to investigate. Key features of the review are included and linked to possible law reform. Further supplementary guidance is also considered. The chapter concludes with a consideration of the law relating to sharing information.

Chapter 2: support and prevention

Support for vulnerable adults may be crucial in preventing abuse. The chapter considers assessment of need for, and provision of, community care services in the context of tightening **eligibility criteria** and the dominant policy of personalization. Risks and benefits of the current policy, which has emerged in the absence of clear legislative underpinning, are discussed, including the concern that **personal assistants** are unregulated and the risk of abuse may be heightened. The chapter continues with discussion of the role of carers, support within mental health law and the position under the Care Act 2014 and its emphasis on well-being.

Chapter 3: criminal law and safeguarding

The role of the criminal law in safeguarding is the focus of this chapter. The range of offences for different types of abuse are outlined, including the offence of ill treatment and wilful neglect of an incapacitated person (as utilized, for example, in the Winterbourne case). Some challenges in the criminal justice system are identified in discussion of the roles of the Crown Prosecution Service (CPS) and the police, evidential issues, and support for vulnerable witnesses and suspects in the context of working with and alongside the police in joint investigations.

Chapter 4: capacity and safeguarding

The relevant provisions within the MCA 2005, informed by the principles of the Act, are considered first. Secondly, the chapter includes specific roles under the Act: deputies, Court of Protection visitors, the Public Guardian and the **Independent Mental Capacity Advocate** (IMCA). The chapter considers the safeguarding relevance of new measures such as **lasting powers of attorney** (LPAs) and DOLS and decisions of the Court of Protection.

Chapter 5: regulation

Regulation contributes to safeguarding with consideration of the role of the CQC, particularly relating to institutional abuse; the vetting and barring scheme established by the Safeguarding Vulnerable Groups Act

2006 as amended by the Protection of Freedoms Act 2012 and role of professional regulatory bodies. Whistleblowing, as a feature of many safeguarding cases in the residential sector and the Public Interest Disclosure Act 1998, is also discussed.

Chapter 6: other legal provision

In addition to the major areas of law outlined above, this chapter will consider aspects of civil law, including tort, contract, undue influence, domestic violence injunctions, law relating to forced marriage, trading standards, powers of entry, and duties under the Equality Act 2010.

Chapter 7: messages from serious case reviews

Safeguarding Adults Boards (SABs) have been established by most local authorities and will be statutorily required once the Care Act 2014 is implemented. The chapter considers their role and membership, including the circumstances in which a safeguarding adults review (SAR) will be called. Current practice has seen a number of serious case reviews and the chapter considers a selection of reviews and the extent to which lessons can be learnt from such reviews.

Chapter 8: conclusion: key developments across the UK

Some concluding thoughts, indication of further law reform and a comparison of the established legislation in Scotland with the new legislation in England and Wales.

Further reading

Journal of Adult Protection (2000 onwards): this specialist journal offers a range of articles with a focus on evidence-based practice in relation to safeguarding adults. Some of the six editions each year are organized around a specific theme and there is a regular legal column.

Mandelstam, M (2011b) *Safeguarding Adults at Risk of Harm: A Legal Guide for Practitioners:* an up-to-date, detailed guide to the law commissioned by the DH, aimed at practitioners.

Mandelstam, M (2013) *Safeguarding Adults and the Law* gives further detail with numerous examples and illustrations of aspects of the law.

Mantell, A and T Scraggs (2011) *Safeguarding Adult's in Social Work.* This book is written with more of a practice focus but with some consideration of the law.

Phelan, A (2013) (ed.) *International Perspectives on Elder Abuse* includes coverage of different conceptualizations of and responses to elder abuse in Australia, Canada, China, Ireland, Israel, Kenya, Latin America, Norway, Spain, the UK and the USA.

Pritchard, J (ed.) (2009) *Good Practice in the Law and Safeguarding Adults: Criminal Justice and Adult Protection* includes some interesting reflections on practice and broad but less detailed coverage of law.

1

GUIDANCE, POLICIES AND PROCEDURES

AT A GLANCE THIS CHAPTER COVERS:

- key guidance on safeguarding adults, *No Secrets*
- discussion of the *No Secrets* review
- the National Framework for Safeguarding Adults
- statement of government policy on adult safeguarding
- Association of Directors of Adult Social Services and Local Government Association advice
- multi-disciplinary working
- communication and sharing information

This chapter focuses on the guidance and direction which is provided for those professionals working in adult safeguarding. In the absence of a central, comprehensive piece of safeguarding legislation, statutory guidance provides the key direction for good practice. The demands of such guidance are great given the complexity of investigations of adult abuse. Penhale and Parker usefully summarize some of the challenges faced by those undertaking an investigation:

> The sensitive nature of the issues involved; matters of capacity, consent, confidentiality and autonomy; continuing challenges presented in the search for effective interdisciplinary working; the absence of a reliable research base on which to sustain practice; the absence of close and effective collaboration linking different policy initiatives such as the tensions that exist between the welfare, legislative and regulatory models of protection.
>
> *Penhale and Parker, 2007:14*

It is perhaps not surprising then that there have been concerns about the content of key guidance, further publications have complemented the original guidance and there have been determined calls for the introduction of legislation rather than reliance on guidance alone. The chapter begins with consideration of the key guidance on adult safeguarding, *No Secrets* (DH, 2000b).

No Secrets: Guidance on Developing and Implementing Multi-agency Policies and Procedures to Protect Vulnerable Adults from Abuse

No Secrets was published in 2000 (DH, 2000b). Equivalent guidance exists in Wales entitled, *In Safe Hands: Implementing Adult Protection Procedures in Wales* (National Assembly for Wales, 2000).

At the outset it is important to recognize the status of *No Secrets*. *No Secrets* is issued under s. 7 Local Authority Social Services Act 1970. The significance of s. 7 guidance was explained by Sedley J in *R v London Borough of Islington ex parte Rixon* [1997]:

> Parliament in enacting section 7(1) did not intend local authorities to whom ministerial guidance was given to be free, having considered it, to take it or leave it ... in my view parliament by s.7(1) has required local authorities to follow the path charted by the Secretary of State's

> guidance, with liberty to deviate from it where the local authority judges on admissible grounds that there is good reason to do so, but without freedom to take a substantially different course.
>
> R v London Borough of Islington ex parte Rixon *[1997] [71]*

Local authorities develop their own policies and procedures drawing heavily on the *No Secrets* guidance, often with additional detail (including timescales), but it is *No Secrets* that provides the legal basis of action. The status of local policy was considered in *R (Lumba) v Secretary of State for the Home Department* [2011]: 'A decision-maker must follow his published policy (and not some different unpublished policy) unless there are good reasons for not doing so.' [16]

Should there be any conflict between statutory guidance and local policy then statutory guidance would be expected to take precedence.

Unusually for s. 7 guidance, *No Secrets* does not specifically attach to a particular statute. Munby LJ remarked on the negative effect of such a position:

> There is the remarkable fact that the formal safeguarding agenda in relation to vulnerable adults rests entirely upon Ministerial guidance and otherwise lacks any statutory basis – a state of affairs that, unsurprisingly, can leave local authorities uncertain as to their function and responsibilities in this vital area. (Munby, 2011:34)

One of the perceived advantages of guidance over legislation is the ease at which it can be revised and amended. Such practice is evident in relation to children where *Working Together to Safeguard Children: A Guide to Inter-Agency Working to Safeguard and Promote the Welfare of Children*, the key statutory guidance under the Children Act 1989, is now in its fifth edition (HM Government, 2013). In contrast, despite considerable practice and legislative changes since 2000, the original version of *No Secrets* still stands and is clearly outdated and inaccurate in some respects. At the same time it would be over-simplistic to suggest that legislation as an alternative to guidance is rigid and does not permit change. Legislation is often drafted in such a way that it can accommodate changes to policy direction. The clearest example of this may prove to be the introduction and existence of personalization in adult social care which has emerged without any changes to the central legislation, the National Health Service and Community Care Act (NHSCCA) 1990. A formal review of *No Secrets* was undertaken in 2008 and is discussed below (DH, 2008a;

2009b). The future of *No Secrets* will now fall to be considered alongside the safeguarding provisions of the Care Act 2014.

Key elements of *No Secrets*

Throughout the text there are references to specific sections of *No Secrets*. This chapter outlines the main features of the guidance in relation to investigations led by the local authority. The overall principles set out in para. 4.3 provide the context for involvement in cases.

Principles

(i) **actively work together** within an inter-agency framework based on the guidance in Section 3;

(ii) **actively promote** the empowerment and well-being of vulnerable adults through the services they provide;

(iii) **act in a way which supports the rights of the individual** to lead an independent life based on self determination and personal choice;

(iv) **recognize people who are unable to take their own decisions** and/or to protect themselves, their assets and bodily integrity;

(v) **recognize that the right to self determination can involve risk** and ensure that such risk is recognized and understood by all concerned, and minimized whenever possible (there should be an open discussion between the individual and the agencies about the risks involved to him or her);

(vi) **ensure the safety of vulnerable adults** by integrating strategies, policies and services relevant to abuse within the framework of the NHS and Community Care Act 1990, the Mental Health Act 1983, the Public Interest Disclosure Act 1998 and the Registered Homes Act 1984 (the provisions of which will be extended by the Care Standards Bill);

(vii) **ensure that when the right to an independent lifestyle and choice is at risk the individual concerned receives appropriate help,** including advice, protection and support from relevant agencies; and

(viii) **ensure that the law and statutory requirements are known and used appropriately** so that vulnerable adults receive the protection of the law and access to the judicial process.

DH, 2000b:4.3 [emphasis in original]

Elements of these principles resonate with other areas of law addressed in the text. For example, working together within an inter-agency framework is supported by the role of Safeguarding Adults Boards (SABs), considered in Chapter 7; promoting empowerment and recognizing that some people are unable to take some decisions is addressed by the MCA 2005, considered in Chapter 4; references to self-determination and personal choice are integral to the policy surrounding personalization as a means of providing support, considered in Chapter 2; and Chapter 5 includes discussion of whistleblowing covered by the Public Interest Disclosure Act 1998 and regulation of residential and other settings, now within the Care Standards Act 2000 which replaced the Registered Homes Act 1984.

Other legislation includes principles which will have an application to some safeguarding cases, notably the principles in the MCA 2005. In addition, when implemented, the principles of the Care Act 2014 will apply across its provisions relating to assessment and services and the provisions relating to safeguarding adults. Section 1(3) sets out a number of matters which might be described as principles to inform practice under the Act. They are contained in the first part of the Act under general responsibilities of the local authority. As well as a specific reference at s. 1(3)(g) to the need to protect people from abuse and neglect, this section applies to the whole of Part 1 of the Act within which the specific safeguarding sections are included.

The Care Act 2014 begins with principles in s. 1:

s. 1

(3) In exercising a function under this Part in the case of an individual, a local authority must have regard to the following matters in particular—
  (a) the importance of beginning with the assumption that the individual is best-placed to judge the individual's well-being;
  (b) the individual's views, wishes and feelings;
  (c) the importance of preventing or delaying the development of needs for care and support or needs for support and the importance of reducing needs of either kind that already exist;
  (d) the need to ensure that decisions about the individual are made having regard to all the individual's circumstances (and are not based only on the individual's age or appearance or any condition of the individual's or aspect of the individual's behaviour which might lead others to make unjustified assumptions about the individual's well-being);

(e) the importance of the individual participating as fully as possible in decisions relating to the exercise of the function concerned and being provided with the information and support necessary to enable the individual to participate;

(f) the importance of achieving a balance between the individual's wellbeing and that of any friends or relatives who are involved in caring for the individual;

(g) the need to protect people from abuse and neglect;

(h) the need to ensure that any restriction on the individual's rights or freedom of action that is involved in the exercise of the function is kept to the minimum necessary for achieving the purpose for which the function is being exercised.

Care Act 2014

Investigation

This document gives guidance to local agencies who have a responsibility to investigate and take action when a vulnerable adult is believed to be suffering abuse. (DH, 2000b:1.5)

Use of the word 'responsibility' in the above paragraph from *No Secrets* is significant. It means that *No Secrets* does not impose a *duty* to investigate. Only legislation could do that. It has been argued that the 'responsibility' to investigate contained in *No Secrets* is effectively upgraded to a duty when considered in conjunction with the Human Rights Act 1998 (Brammer, 2010). The Act of course, in s. 6, states that it is 'unlawful for a public authority to act in a way which is incompatible with a Convention right'. The early case of *X and Y v The Netherlands* (1985) clearly confirmed that the sexual abuse of a young woman with a learning disability constituted a breach of her right to respect for private and family life. Further, if abuse meets the threshold in Article 3 ECHR as constituting inhuman or degrading treatment, there is a positive obligation on the state to offer protection, beyond investigation. Positive obligations also arise in connection with Articles 2 and 8 ECHR. Whilst this reasoning may be correct, it is somewhat tortuous and a poor substitute for a clear statutory duty. Responses to the *Review of No Secrets* (DH, 2008a; 2009b) and to the Law Commission (2010; 2011) expressed concern that this was a major weakness of the framework for adult safeguarding and in contrast to the clear duty to investigate suspicions of significant harm to children under the Children Act 1989.

Implementation of the Care Act 2014 will resolve this deficiency by s. 42:

s. 42 Enquiry by local authority

(1) This section applies where a local authority has reasonable cause to suspect that an adult in its area (whether or not ordinarily resident there)—

    (a) has needs for care and support (whether or not the authority is meeting any of those needs),

    (b) is experiencing, or is at risk of, abuse or neglect, and

    (c) as a result of those needs is unable to protect himself or herself against the abuse or neglect or the risk of it.

(2) The local authority **must** [emphasis added] make (or cause to be made) whatever enquiries it thinks necessary to enable it to decide whether any action should be taken in the adult's case (whether under this Part or otherwise) and, if so, what and by whom.

Care Act 2014

The important word there is *must* which denotes a duty to make (or cause to be made) enquiries. There is a link between the duty to make enquiries and assessment for support. The Care Act 2014 provides that, where an individual refuses an assessment, the local authority will not be required to carry it out except where:

s. 11(2)

    (a) the adult lacks capacity to refuse the assessment and the authority is satisfied that carrying out the assessment would be in the adult's best interests, or

    (b) the adult is experiencing, or is at risk of, abuse or neglect.

Care Act 2014

Returning to *No Secrets* (DH, 2000b), the objectives of an investigation are set out at para 6.3 as to:

- establish facts;
- assess the needs of the vulnerable adult for protection, support and redress; and
- make decisions with regard to what follow-up action should be taken with regard to the perpetrator and the service or its management if they have been culpable, ineffective or negligent.

At para. 6.13 the stages of an investigation are set out:

- **reporting** to a single referral point;
- **recording,** with sensitivity to the abused person, the precise factual details of the alleged abuse;
- **initial co-ordination** involving representatives of all agencies which might have a role in a subsequent investigation and could constitute a strategy meeting;
- **investigation** within a jointly determined framework to determine the facts of the case; and
- **decision making** which may take place at a shared forum such as a case conference.

DH, 2000b:6.13 [emphasis in original]

From this guidance local authorities have developed their own policies and procedures which usually provide additional detail to the bare framework outlined, such as the calling and conduct of case conferences or timescales for each stage of the investigation.

Allegations of abuse will trigger the investigative procedure. *No Secrets* refers to making an assessment of seriousness to justify intervention in terms of: the vulnerability of the individual; nature and extent of the abuse; length of time it has been occurring; impact on the individual; and risk of repetition or increasingly serious acts (DH, 2000b:2.19). These considerations might be described as a threshold for intervention, however, *No Secrets* provides no guidance on the stage before intervention when initial consideration of referrals/allegations are made.

ADASS and LGA (2013b) note that reports of concerns have increased alongside greater awareness of adult abuse. There is a worry that some concerns are routed into safeguarding when in fact alternative routes would have been appropriate, e.g. disciplinary proceedings. It is now common practice for authorities to have referral thresholds that distinguish between initial alerts, which should be logged and may be referred to other organizations, and those which proceed as safeguarding referrals. An obvious concern with such a system is that thresholds for recognizing a concern as a safeguarding matter may vary between authorities.

> **KEY CASE ANALYSIS** ←

Davis and Davis v West Sussex County Council [2012]

The case concerned a safeguarding investigation into alleged abuse at Nyton House care home, West Sussex. The claimants, Mary and Philip Davis (owners of the care home) applied for decisions made by West Sussex County Council at a safeguarding vulnerable adults case conference to be quashed on the basis that they were made in breach of rules of natural justice, government guidance (*No Secrets* (DH, 2000b)), the council's own policies and a legitimate expectation. The claim that council contractual arrangements with the home took precedence over *No Secrets* was firmly rejected.

As a judicial review, the focus of the court was on the decision-making process rather than the substance of the allegations. The case came to the attention of the council as a result of a whistleblowing alert raising concern that some procedures (dressing cuts and wounds and ear-syringing) were being undertaken by care staff and should properly have been left to the community nursing service. The facts of the case are detailed and it is worth reading the law report in full.

Key elements of the case included that: the claimants were not aware until August of police involvement as lead investigators since May; they received insufficient notice of allegations and were not shown evidence against them; the case conference was not shown any evidence; the claimants were not permitted to produce relevant evidence to the case conference. Although there were many failings in the case, the judge acknowledged the difficulties faced by professionals working in adult safeguarding:

> As I have been critical of West Sussex I repeat my view that the professionals in this case acted throughout in good faith and having in mind the best interests of those they are engaged to protect. There are obviously great pressures on local authority employees carrying out this important and stressful work. The consequences of a failure to intervene can be grave. Those working in this area face criticism for allegedly interfering when they intervene and for alleged neglect or worse when they do not. [101]

The significance of the case is that, whilst safeguarding processes have been the subject of local government ombudsman investigations, this is the first High Court decision to consider the role of the *No Secrets* guidance in safeguarding practice.

National Framework for Safeguarding Adults

In 2005, ADSS published *Safeguarding Adults: A National Framework of Standards for Good Practice and Outcomes in Adult Protection Work* (the National Framework for Safeguarding Adults). The framework comprises 11 standards for good practice in safeguarding adults. This document saw the formal introduction of the term 'safeguarding' in an adult context, in preference to vulnerable adult and adult protection, explaining further:

> This phrase means all work which enables an adult 'who is or may be eligible for community care services' to retain independence, wellbeing and choice and to access their human right to live a life that is free from abuse and neglect. This definition specifically includes those people who are assessed as being able to purchase all or part of their community care services, as well as those who are eligible for community care services but whose need – in relation to safeguarding – is for access to mainstream services such as the police.
>
> *ADSS, 2005:5*

It also made connections with the MCA 2005 and recognized that principles in that Act would have an application in and inform safeguarding cases, including, importantly, the principles that adults with capacity can make 'unwise' decisions, and any decisions taken on behalf of an adult who lacked capacity had to be in their '**best interests**' and the least intrusive option.

The standards are:

> **Standard 1** Each local authority has established a multi-agency partnership to lead 'Safeguarding Adults' work.
>
> **Standard 2** Accountability for and ownership of 'Safeguarding Adults' work is recognised by each partner organisation's executive body.
>
> **Standard 3** The 'Safeguarding Adults' policy includes a clear statement of every person's right to live a life free from abuse and neglect, and this message is actively promoted to the public by the Local Strategic Partnership, the 'Safeguarding Adults' partnership, and its member organisations.
>
> **Standard 4** Each partner agency has a clear, well-publicised policy of Zero-Tolerance of abuse within the organisation.
>
> **Standard 5** The 'Safeguarding Adults' partnership oversees a multi-agency workforce development/training sub-group. The partnership has

a workforce development/training strategy and ensures that it is appropriately resourced.

Standard 6 All citizens can access information about how to gain safety from abuse and violence, including information about the local 'Safeguarding Adults' procedures.

Standard 7 There is a local multi-agency 'Safeguarding Adults' policy and procedure describing the framework for responding to all adults *'who is or may be eligible for community care services'* **and** who may be at risk of abuse or neglect. [original emphasis]

Standard 8 Each partner agency has a set of internal guidelines, consistent with the local multi-agency 'Safeguarding Adults' policy and procedures, which set out the responsibilities of all workers to operate within it.

Standard 9 The multi-agency 'Safeguarding Adults' procedures detail the following stages: Alert, Referral, Decision, Safeguarding assessment strategy, Safeguarding assessment, Safeguarding plan, Review, Recording and Monitoring.

Standard 10 The safeguarding procedures are accessible to all adults covered by the policy.

Standard 11 The partnership explicitly includes service users as key partners in all aspects of the work. This includes building service-user participation into its: membership; monitoring, development and implementation of its work; training strategy; and planning and implementation of their individual safeguarding assessment and plans.

ADSS, 2005:3

The standards are accompanied by sub-objectives and the guide includes examples of good practice and illustrative scenarios.

Review of *No Secrets*

A review of *No Secrets* was introduced by the following statement:

Seven years on, and in the light of several serious incidences of adult abuse, it is timely to review this guidance and to consult with other government departments ... New guidance is necessary to reflect the evidence in today's report and respond to the new demographic realities which are affecting our society. We will also consider the case for legislation as part of the review process.

DH, 2008a

In terms of its timing, the review was prompted by a number of factors. Since 2000 there have been major changes in the policy environment, including the commitment to personalization. Weaknesses in the implementation of *No Secrets* had been identified, including inconsistent implementation across the country. A third prompt was the need to examine the case for legislative change given the identified lack of legislative provision compared to that in existence for safeguarding children. A review of the Welsh equivalent to *No Secrets*, entitled, *In Safe Hands*, also took place (National Assembly for Wales, 2000).

Messages that emerged from the consultation supported revision of *No Secrets* and some statutory changes. A key emphasis of responses was the need to hear the voice of vulnerable people. That voice is evident in the four key messages identified in the document, namely: safeguarding requires empowerment – hearing the victim's voice; empowerment is everybody's business, but safeguarding decisions are not; safeguarding adults is not like child protection – there are differences; and participation/representation of people who lack capacity is also important (DH, 2008a).

Specific questions focused on the need for statutory reform. A significant proportion of respondents, 68 per cent (of written responses) were absolutely in support of new legislation, with a further 11 per cent answering 'maybe' or making further suggestions. Support for legislation at the consultation events was described as 'widespread and vociferous' (DH, 2009b:91). Arguments cited in favour of legislation were grouped into four themes. Firstly, a desire to mirror child protection, not necessarily in the detail but in the fact that the arrangements for safeguarding children, including underpinning principles, are rooted in legislation. A second theme concerned the impact that legislation might have on practice. It was argued that legislation would raise the priority given to safeguarding, make multi-agency working more effective and could carry more resources into this area of work. The link between the first two themes was nicely summarized by McKeough:

> There remains an urgent need for legislation that puts adult protection on a similar footing to the statutory model of child protection and puts out the signal that the abuse of an adult is as serious as the abuse of a child. Such an approach will help increase the status of adult protection work within health and social care organisations ...
>
> *McKeough, 2009:9*

Thirdly, it was noted that legislation exists in Scotland, in the form of the Adult Support and Protection (Scotland) Act 2007, and it was argued that similar provision should be introduced in England. The fourth theme acknowledged the change in policy in adult social care, referred to as the choice agenda, and the need to balance increased individual choice which may carry increased risks of harm, with safeguarding measures.

Certain of those arguments were dismissed by those respondents opposed to the introduction of legislation. There was some recognition of the progress made in adult safeguarding without legislation and also some critique of elements of the framework for safeguarding children, including its bureaucracy and the fact that different values apply to adults than to (in particular) young children, who are unable to give consent. The role of legislation was questioned, with some arguing that new legislation would not raise the priority of adult safeguarding and use of existing legislation would be sufficient. There were some concerns about the content of the Scottish legislation and reluctance to follow that line in the absence of an evaluation into its operation. Finally, whilst the need to balance the choice and safeguarding agendas was recognized, some felt that legislation would not achieve this, arguing that safeguarding is most effective when it is a mainstream activity (including commissioning, assessment and housing work).

The next stage in the development of policy on adult safeguarding followed the election of the new Coalition government.

Statement of government policy on adult safeguarding

In May 2011, the Coalition government issued a statement of its policy on adult safeguarding (DH, 2011b). It includes a number of principles which may be translated into outcomes, by which agencies are invited to benchmark their existing safeguarding arrangements:

- empowerment: presumption of person-led decisions and informed consent;
- protection: support and representation for those in greatest need;
- prevention: better to take action before harm occurs;
- **proportionality**: proportionate and least intrusive response appropriate to risk presented;
- partnership: local solutions through services working with their communities – preventing, detecting and reporting neglect and abuse;

- accountability: accountability and transparency in delivering safe-guarding.

The document status is described as building on *No Secrets* which is to remain as the statutory guidance until at least 2015. A key feature of the policy is a commitment to legislate to make SABs statutory, as also recommended by the Law Commission.

Safeguarding Adults: Advice and Guidance to Directors of Adult Social Services

Most recently the ADASS and LGA published an advice note to Directors of Adult Social Services (ADASS and LGA, 2013b), which it describes as complementing *No Secrets* (DH, 2000b), the National Framework for Safeguarding Adults (ADSS, 2005) and the 'Statement of government policy' (DH, 2011b).

The advice note recognizes the changing landscape of adult safe-guarding, including likely legislative change and the impact of high profile scandals and asserts that 'safeguarding adults is one of the highest priorities for Councils and will remain so' (ADASS and LGA, 2013b:3).

Key messages for directors, and hence for practice are:

- focus on people and the outcomes they want;
- collaborative leadership – supporting, integrating and holding part-ners to account;
- effective interfaces with developing Health and Wellbeing Boards, Community Safety Partnerships, Safeguarding Children Boards;
- responsive specialist services to support people with difficult decision-making;
- making sure concerns are addressed proportionately so that systems are not swamped and really serious concerns are not missed;
- commissioning, contracts management, care management review and safeguarding intelligence are fully integrated.

Priority areas for directors are: achieving good outcomes for service users; responding to reported abuse; leadership; and SABs.

Other important sources of guidance are the Codes of Practice issued alongside the Mental Capacity Act 2005 and Mental Health Act 1983, discussed further in Chapter 4.

Multi-disciplinary working

As discussed above, *No Secrets* (DH, 2000b) carries a particular status for social services as guidance issued under s. 7 Local Authority Social Services Act 1970. It clearly envisages multi-disciplinary working but with responsibility for coordinating with the local social services authority as lead agency. It is commended to health professionals, the police, criminal justice agencies and regulators, etc., but it is not issued to those bodies under an equivalent to s. 7. All relevant agencies are expected to have a designated lead officer for safeguarding and to work together in partnership with each other and 'in collaboration with all agencies involved in the public, voluntary and private sectors and they should also consult service users, their carers and representative groups' (para 1.3). *No Secrets* is thus intended to have an impact on a wider range of agencies than the statutory core agencies (social services, health, police). The range of agencies envisaged by *No Secrets* is set out at para 3.3, namely:

- commissioners of health and social care services;
- providers of health and social care services;
- providers of sheltered and supported housing;
- regulators of services;
- the police and other relevant law enforcement agencies (including the CPS);
- voluntary and private sector agencies;
- other local authority departments, e.g. housing and education;
- probation departments;
- Department of Social Security benefit agencies;
- carer support groups;
- user groups and user-led services;
- advocacy and advisory services;
- community safety partnerships;
- services meeting the needs of specific groups experiencing violence;
- and agencies offering legal advice and representation.

No Secrets also recognized that: 'To achieve effective inter-agency working, agencies may consider that there are merits in establishing a multi-agency management committee (adult protection).' (para 3.4) In practice SABs exist in most areas and often mirror Local Children Safeguarding Boards in their make-up and objectives. A statutory obligation to establish such boards is to be introduced under the Care Act 2014. The role of SABs is discussed in more detail in Chapter 7.

Support for partnership working relating to adult safeguarding may be gleaned from other sources. For example, the Carers (Equal Opportunities) Act 2004 encourages a multi-disciplinary approach to carer support but does not mandate cooperation. The local authority may request the assistance of other bodies in planning provision of services to carers and cared for persons and can also request the other body to provide a service if that would enhance the carers' ability to provide care. Other local authorities, social services departments, local education authorities, housing and NHS bodies are included as 'other bodies'. In either case the body should give 'due consideration' to the request. In times of limited resources, however, such a weakly expressed requirement may remain aspirational.

Collaborative work is essential to secure a timely and coordinated response to safeguarding concerns. Regrettably, lack of or ineffective sharing of information has been a feature of both child and adult serious case reviews. A duty to cooperate imposed on bodies likely to be represented on safeguarding boards may strengthen inter-agency working within a framework of accountability to the board, and give teeth to the *No Secrets* call for 'all responsible agencies [to] work together to ensure … a consistent and effective response to any circumstances giving ground for concern' (DH, 2000:1.2).

Looking forward, the Care Act 2014 contains provisions on cooperation between agencies which will apply to the safeguarding provisions and to assessment for support. Section 45 deals with the specific circumstance of supplying information to SABs and is considered in Chapter 7.

Section 6 covers cooperating generally. A local authority must cooperate with each of its relevant partners, and each relevant partner must cooperate with the authority, in the exercise of functions relating to adults with needs for care and support and carers. It must also make arrangements to ensure cooperation between officers with functions relating to adults with needs for care and support and carers (broadly speaking this will be social services) with housing, the Director of Children's Services at the authority and the authority's Director of Public Health.

The following purposes of such cooperation are detailed as:

s. 6(6)

- promoting the well-being of adults with needs for care and support and of carers;

- improving the quality of care and support for adults and support for carers;
- smoothing the transition to the system provided for by this Part for persons in relation to whom functions under ss 58 to 65 are exercisable;
- protecting adults with needs for care and support who are experiencing, or are at risk of, abuse or neglect; and
- identifying lessons to be learned from cases where adults with needs for care and support have experienced serious abuse or neglect and applying those lessons to future cases.

Care Act 2014

Relevant partners of a local authority include: district councils; any other authority it agrees to cooperate with; NHS bodies in the area; the police, prisons and probation services; and others specified by regulations. Under s. 7, in specific cases where the authority requests cooperation of a partner in the exercise of functions relating to an individual with needs for care and support or a carer of a child or a young carer, the partner or authority must comply unless it would be incompatible with its own duties, or otherwise have an adverse effect on the exercise of its functions. Written reasons must be given for decisions not to comply.

Sharing information

The legality of sharing information is governed by principles of confidentiality and key legislation – the Data Protection Act 1998 and Freedom of Information Act 2000. It is important to appreciate that these principles provide a framework for safe and responsible information-sharing in safeguarding cases, although sometimes they may be misunderstood and fear of breaching confidentiality may circumscribe good practice. Serious case reviews have consistently identified the need for better information-sharing. Standard 6 (ADSS, 2005) stresses the importance of an information-sharing protocol between agencies.

Confidentiality

A duty of confidence attaches to certain relationships including a range of professionals and their clients, e.g. doctor and patient, solicitor and client, social worker and client. The British Association of Social Workers' (BASW) *Code of Ethics* (2012) requires social workers to respect principles of confidentiality. Without an expectation of confidence many clients would feel inhibited and unwilling to discuss personal issues and it is appropriate to give an assurance that information will be treated as confidential unless certain circumstances arise. An absolute guarantee of confidence should not be given. Where it is appropriate to share information, care needs to be taken to ensure compliance with **data protection** rules and to share effectively with agencies that genuinely need to know.

Confidential information may be shared in the following circumstances:

- where the individual gives consent;
- under s. 115 Crime and Disorder Act 1998, relevant authorities may disclose information when it is necessary or expedient for the purposes of the Act including the prevention of crime and disorder;
- a duty to disclose information is contained in other specific legislation, e.g. the Police and Criminal Evidence Act 1984;
- public interest may outweigh the individual's interest in maintaining confidentiality;
- court proceedings require disclosure of all relevant material but this will not be disclosed beyond the parties to the case without the permission of the court;
- interest of the subject, as expressed in the *No Secrets* requirement to, 'balance the requirements of confidentiality with the consideration that, to protect vulnerable adults, it may be necessary to share information on a "need-to-know basis"' (DH, 2000b:3.6).

Any decision to share information should be recorded, identifying the precise information to be shared and the justification for sharing.

The Data Protection Act 1998

The Data Protection Act 1998 addresses the ways data is processed and introduced the right of an individual to request information held about them. Key definitions under the Act include:

- *data*: a broad term including electronic and handwritten records;
- *personal data*: information from which a living person can be identified;
- *sensitive personal data*: information on racial or ethnic origin, political opinion, religious or similar beliefs, trade union membership, physical or mental health condition, sexual life, actual or alleged criminal activity;

- *data processing*: obtaining, recording, holding or carrying out any operation on data – this includes any use of data, its disclosure and destruction;
- *subject access right*: the right of the individual (data subject) to ask for a copy of information held about them by a person or organization.

There are eight data protection principles which should be integrated into practice (See Schedule 1).

Data protection principles

1 Personal data must be processed fairly and lawfully.
2 Personal data shall only be obtained for specific lawful purposes and must not be processed in any way incompatible with that purpose.
3 Personal data must be adequate, relevant and not excessive for the purpose for which it is collected.
4 Personal data shall be accurate and kept up to date when necessary.
5 Personal data must be kept no longer than necessary.
6 Personal data shall be processed in accordance with the rights of data subjects.
7 Appropriate measures shall be taken against any unlawful processing of personal data or accidental loss, damage or destruction of personal data.
8 Personal data shall not be transferred outside the European Economic Area unless the country to which it is transferred has an equivalent type of data protection law.

A request for personal data may be refused in certain circumstances, including: where the information identifies other people; where disclosure of information is likely to cause serious harm to the physical or mental health of the data subject or any other person; and where disclosure of the information would be prejudicial to the prevention or detection of crime or arrest or prosecution of offenders.

The Freedom of Information Act 2000 is also relevant to recorded information on safeguarding. The Act applies to public authorities, including local and national government, and introduces a right of access to information held by authorities in carrying out their public functions. There are exemptions including personal information, court records and information provided in confidence. As an example, a person could legitimately request information on the number of safeguarding adults referrals a local authority received in the course of a year. Information relating to the identification of the subjects of those referrals, however, would be exempt.

On-the-spot question	Consider the impact of the Data Protection Act 1998 and Freedom of Information Act 2000 on social work record-keeping. Has the legislation had a positive effect?

Recording skills

No Secrets notes:

> Whenever a complaint or allegation of abuse is made all agencies should keep clear and accurate records **and each agency should identify procedures for incorporating,** on receipt of a complaint or allegation, all relevant agency and service user records into a file to record all action taken. (DH, 2000b:6.14) [original emphasis]

Whilst agencies will have their own preferences in style, format and use of technology, accurate and detailed record-keeping is an essential feature of good practice in safeguarding adults (Pritchard and Leslie, 2011). Record-keeping is an aspect of accountability and consideration of records is an important element of supervision. Ultimately, records may become evidence in court proceedings and can be the difference between securing the desired outcome in a case or not. Some key points are set out below.

Essentials of good record-keeping

- Ensure records are relevant, accurate and impartial.
- Records should begin with an account of the first alert or referral.
- Records should be dated.
- Recording should take place contemporaneously with the event or as soon as possible afterwards.
- Distinguish between fact and opinion.
- Record decisions made and their basis i.e. factors taken into account – consider use of a balance sheet.
- Keep an up-to-date chronology.
- Record contact with other agencies and information shared.

- Record advice sought from line managers/lawyers.
- Be aware of who might read your records – including your client.
- Know your agency policy on storage and archiving of records.
- Hand-written records should be legible.
- Use punctuation appropriately, including quotation marks.
- A genogram may be useful in a complex family.
- Explain acronyms.

PRACTICE FOCUS

Susan attends a day centre and has told one of the staff, Helen, that she thinks her brother is stealing money from her parents. She asks Helen not to tell anyone as she is scared of her brother. Helen assures Susan that her secret is safe with her. She makes a note in Susan's file stating that Susan is obviously unhappy at home and not getting on with her brother. The note is not dated or signed. In supervision she repeats what Susan told her about her brother and states that she did not record the comment as it was told to her in confidence.

- What concerns arise in this scenario?

Further reading

DH (2000a) *Data Protection Act 1998: Guidance to Social Services* provides details of the data protection framework.

DH (2008a) *Safeguarding Adults: A Review of the 'No Secrets' Guidance*

DH (2009b) *Safeguarding Adults: Report on the Consultation on the Review of No Secrets – Guidance on Developing and Implementing Multi-agency Policies and Procedures to Protect Vulnerable Adults from Abuse* in relation to the *No Secrets* review.

Hewitt, D (2013) 'Her treatment at and around the meeting was deplorable: might safeguarding itself constitute abuse?' 15(2) *Journal of Adult Protection* 96. This article examines the *Davis* case.

HM Government (2008) *Information Sharing: Guidance for Practitioners and Managers* includes a checklist of seven questions to help with decision-making on sharing information.

Hobbs, A and A Alonzi (2013) 'Mediation and family group conferences in adult safeguarding' 15(2) *Journal of Adult Protection* 69 considers multi-agency working.

Minister of State (2010) *Government Response to the Consultation on Safeguarding Adults: The Review of the No Secrets Guidance* also in relation to the *No Secrets* review.

Pinkney, L, B Penhale, J Manthorpe, N Perkins, D Reid and S Hussein (2008) 'Voices from the frontline: social work practitioners' perceptions of multi-agency working in adult protection in England and Wales' 10(4) *Journal of Adult Protection* 12–23 also considers multi-agency working.

2
SUPPORT AND PREVENTION

AT A GLANCE THIS CHAPTER COVERS:

- *No Secrets'* emphasis on prevention
- raising awareness
- community care services and eligibility criteria
- personalization
- support provisions within mental health law
- role of carers
- transitions and leaving care
- Care Act 2014 and 'well-being'

A commitment to the least intrusive intervention in safeguarding entails early consideration of preventive measures and support services (SCIE, 2011). This chapter focuses on the concept of support as a means of preventing initial or further abuse. Support may be provided to the actual or potential victim and to the perpetrator of abuse. In many cases the relationship may include a caring role and an element of mutual dependence and it would be inappropriate to focus solely on the needs of one person. The emphasis on preventing abuse is clearly stated in *No Secrets*:

> agencies' primary aim should be to prevent abuse where possible but, if the preventive strategy fails, agencies should ensure that robust procedures are in place for dealing with incidents of abuse (DH, 2000b:1.2).

The legal framework for the provision of support is acknowledged as complex, confusing and outdated (Law Commission, 2008) and is undergoing major transformation with the introduction of the Care Act 2014. The piecemeal development of the law since 1948 has resulted in duplication and inconsistency and the opportunity to reform and consolidate the law is welcome. Given the timescales involved in implementing new legislation it is necessary to begin with consideration of the existing law which will continue in force until the reform process is complete. The concluding section of the chapter outlines the provisions of the Care Act 2014, recognizing that, until rules, regulations, guidance and codes are published the picture is incomplete.

The key legislation under which needs for support are assessed is the NHSCCA 1990. True commitment to prevention requires necessary resources and much of the case law discussed in this chapter concerns allocation of limited resources. The ways in which support is provided have changed and expanded with the advent of personalization policy. The *No Secrets* review (discussed in Chapter 1: DH, 2008a; 2009b) noted the importance of achieving balance between the aims of safeguarding and increased independence with personalization.

Legal reform of this area is long overdue. There are wider concerns, however, as noted by CQC (2013b), recognizing that the increasing trend for people being cared for in their own homes is likely to continue, as will the growth in provision of home care services. The CQC report, *Not Just a Number*, reports on the inspection of 250 home care services, ranging in size from those providing care for fewer than five people to the largest organization providing care for over 700. Characteristics of good care included: good written information and face-to-face explanations of available services and choices; involvement of carers and relatives in care; individuals being encouraged to express their views; care plans being kept up to date; and staff only undertaking tasks for which they have necessary knowledge and skills. Concerns fell into five main groups: late and missed calls; lack of consistency of workers; lack of support for staff and issues around travel time; incomplete records and ineffective complaints; and poor understanding of safeguarding.

O'Keefe et al. (2007) found that particular types of abuse were more likely in private settings, namely, neglect, financial abuse and interpersonal abuse. Individuals may receive intimate care within situations where there is no external scrutiny and the risk is effectively hidden (Cambridge et al., 2000).

Provision of support and information may also enable and empower the individual to report and challenge abuse. Public awareness campaigns can contribute to the preventative agenda though it is difficult to detect a consistent strategy for raising awareness other than through the work of organizations such as Action on Elder Abuse and, perhaps indirectly, via the publication of and surrounding media interest in the Francis Report into events at Mid Staffordshire hospital (Francis, 2010). Developing personal strategies for self-protection are also important (Bruder and Kroese, 2005; Hollomotoz, 2011).

As with many aspects of practice inter-agency collaboration is essential. Regulation also has a central role, including setting and enforcing standards of good care across settings and ensuring unsuitable people do not work with vulnerable adults (see further discussion in Chapter 5).

Prevention is a broad term and, in the context of adult safeguarding, Kalaga and Kingston's model is helpful. They identify three levels of intervention:

- primary interventions: aim to prevent abuse occurring in the first instance;
- secondary interventions: aim to identify and respond directly to allegations of abuse;
- tertiary interventions: aim to remedy any negative and harmful consequences of abuse and to put in place measures to prevent future occurrences. (Kalaga and Kingston, 2007: cited in SCIE, 2011:4)

A Commission for Social Care Inspection (CSCI) (2008) summary of key elements for prevention and early intervention expands on ways such interventions may manifest:

- people being informed of their rights to be free from abuse and supported to exercise these rights, including access to advocacy;
- a well-trained workforce operating in a culture of zero tolerance of abuse;
- a sound framework for confidentiality and information-sharing across agencies;
- good universal services, such as community safety services;
- needs and risk assessments to inform people's choices;
- a range of options for support to keep safe from abuse tailored to people's individual needs;
- services that prioritize both safeguarding and independence; and
- public awareness of the issues.

The consequences of failing to provide support may be grave, resulting in deterioration of a situation until it reaches potentially life-threatening levels. It may also breach human rights. In *R (Bernard) v Enfield London Borough Council* [2003], community care services identified in an assessment of need were not provided and this violated Article 8 ECHR, the right to respect for private and family life. The positive obligation to promote Article 8 rights should be a key consideration in the provision of support (Ellis, 2004).

Community care

Direct local authority provision of services, once the norm, is now relatively unusual. The purchaser/provider split means that local authorities are involved in commissioning services from the independent, private and voluntary sectors. The terms of these contracting arrangements provide the potential to ensure that the local authority prioritizes safeguarding with the actual providers of services. Many factors beyond cost should influence the local authority choice to commission services from a particular provider.

The starting point for assessing and meeting need for support services is s. 47 NHSCCA 1990. Full consideration of community care law is provided in a range of specialist texts (Butler, 2012; Clements and Thompson, 2011). In essence, s. 47 imposes a duty on local authorities to carry out an assessment of need for anyone with an appearance of need for services. This duty is followed by a power, having regard to the results of the assessment, to decide whether the needs will be met by the provision of services.

Eligibility criteria

A structure for the discretionary element of s. 47 NHSCCA 1990 is now provided by guidance. The significant decision of *R v Gloucestershire County Council ex parte Barry* [1997] established the principle that local authorities could take into account as a relevant factor their financial resources in decisions about allocation of community care services. Such allocation must be in a structured fashion and local authority eligibility criteria were introduced as a result. Fair access to care services guidance (DH, 2003; 2010) attempted to achieve consistency across local authority boundaries in rationing resources by introducing four eligibility bands for the assessment of need – critical, substantial, moderate and low.

In relation to abuse the critical band includes 'serious abuse or neglect has occurred/will occur'. The role of actual or potential carers may be considered under the critical band statement: 'Vital social support systems and relationships cannot/will not be sustained.' In the substantial band there is reference to abuse or neglect. In practice most authorities only meet needs in the critical and substantial band, confirmed as lawful practice in *R (Chavda) v Harrow London Borough Council* [2007], and indeed some only meet needs in the critical band. It is difficult to reconcile this reality with a preventative aspiration. For some individuals it will be a case of waiting for inevitable deterioration in their circumstances before support will be provided. Further, if services are required due to concerns about abuse or neglect, and authorities only meet critical needs, that will involve an assessment of seriousness, in effect a high threshold for support.

The actual service provision following assessment under s. 47 has to be drawn from pre-existing legislation and is collectively defined as 'community care services' by s. 46(3) NHSCCA 1990. Increasingly, individuals will receive a personal budget with choice and control as to how it is spent, rather than direct provision of services. A mechanism commonly utilized to calculate the amount of the personal budget is the Resource Allocation System (RAS), both are discussed in the context of personalization below.

→ KEY CASE ANALYSIS ←

R (McDonald) v Kensington and Chelsea Royal London Borough Council [2011]

Ms McDonald, a former ballerina, needed to urinate several times a night and required assistance to get to the commode or bathroom. She was not incontinent. Originally, her care package provided a carer overnight to assist with mobility. This was very expensive. The council proposed to replace that service with the provision of continence pads and sheeting. It reframed the original assessment of 'need for assistance to use the commode at night' with a more broadly worded 'need to urinate safely at night'. The Court of Appeal found that, from the review of needs onwards, the council was justified in meeting the expressed need by provision of continence aids. This view was upheld by the Supreme Court, with a powerful dissenting view from LJ Hale (George, 2011; Carr, 2012). The majority ruled that Article 8 ECHR rights were not breached, any interference was proportionate as a means of ensuring her safety and independence and promoting equitable allocation of limited resources. Such a stance clearly upholds the established position that a local authority has a discretion as to how to meet individual needs and, in doing so, it can take resources into account. Lady Hale did not dispute this principle, but did argue that the provision of continence pads did not meet her needs and a logical extension of the argument would entitle the authority to withdraw support during the day as well as night. Not surprisingly, the judgment has received criticism for its apparent failure to recognize dignity (Clements, 2011b).

Human rights considerations, Article 8 ECHR in particular, have featured in other community care cases. *A v East Sussex County Council* [2003] centred on a dispute about manual handling for two severely disabled sisters. The judgment includes a number of more positive statements about the application of Article 8 ECHR (right to respect for private and family life) to disabled people.

The other important concept embraced in the 'physical and psychological integrity' protected by Article 8 is the right of the disabled person to participate in the life of the community and to have what has been described as 'access to essential economic and social activities and to an appropriate range of recreational and cultural activities'. This is matched by the positive obligation of the state to take appropriate measures designed to ensure to the greatest extent feasible that a disabled person is not 'so circumscribed and so isolated as to be deprived of the possibility of developing his personality'.

Personalization

The concept of personalization dominates the policy and practice of service provision. Clements (2011c) notes that 'in contrast to the many statutory duties and the fanfare of regulations that underpin community care law, personalisation is based on no law whatsoever'. It is true that there is no direct reference to personalization within legislation and no 'Personalization Act'. In truth, the legal foundations of personalization remain the NHSCCA 1990 and associated legislation, particularly that which provides for direct payments. It is difficult to precisely define personalization and it is likely to remain a fluid term. A formal description can be found in *Transforming Adult Social Care:*

> What it means is that everyone who receives social care support, regardless of their level of need, in any setting, whether from statutory services, the third and community or private sector or by funding it themselves, will have choice and control over how that support is delivered. It will mean that people are able to live their own lives as they wish, confident that services are of high quality, are safe and promote their own individual requirements for independence, well-being and dignity.
>
> *DH, 2008:4*

Within the broad policy of personalization, various terminology is in play, including individual or personal budgets and self-directed support. Direct payments were introduced by the Community Care (Direct Payments) Act 1996 and enabled individuals to choose and purchase services. Initially, payments would only be made if the individual could consent and manage the payment themselves. The Health and Social Care Act 2008 amended the law so that payments could be made to a 'suitable person', thereby allowing people previously excluded from direct payments, e.g. some with learning disabilities, to benefit from the policy. The proportion of people who take their personal budget as a direct payment is on the increase, from 11.7 per cent in 2010/2011 to 16.4 per cent in 2012/2013 (HSCIC, 2013).

A personal budget is not synonymous with a direct payment. It is an allocation or budget, sufficient to meet assessed need, which may be taken as direct payments or used by the council or a budget broker to flexibly meet the care plan objectives for the individual. Although this is an accepted practice, according to *R (Broster and Others) v Wirrall Metropolitan Borough Council* [2010], there is no duty on a local authority to provide a personal budget and a refusal to do so does not breach Article 8 ECHR or equality legislation. In this case, personal budgets were not provided to 16 people with learning disabilities, living as tenants of an organization providing accommodation and services under contract to the council. The court was concerned that the tenants would be unduly influenced by the organization in deciding to spend their budget allocation with that organization even after the council withdrew from the contract.

The RAS is used by many local authorities in conjunction with personal budgets. It is a mechanism which sets indicative allocations for the cost of meeting specific need. The RAS does not replace the role of assessors, however, it is to be used as a starting point for a determination of a personal budget which an assessor must then consider. This was the outcome of *R (Raphaela Savva) v Kensington and Chelsea* [2010] in which a disabled woman challenged use of the RAS to calculate her personal budget. The Court of Appeal confirmed that the council could use the RAS as a starting point but that it must also give an adequate explanation of how a personal budget allocation is determined. Further, in *R (KM) v Cambridgeshire County Council* [2010], the RAS was used as a starting point, adjusted by a practitioner's assessment.

Personal assistants

A direct payment may be used to employ a personal assistant (PA). An advantage of this development is that the individual has a free choice as to whom they employ and may be able to use direct payments to secure involvement of a friend or carer for some remuneration. A potential disadvantage is that PAs are not included within the vetting and barring scheme and not subject to any formal regulation and there is no obligation to undertake criminal records checks. Recruitment of the right person can be a concern (Flynn, 2005), although it is possible to appoint somebody already known to the individual. DH guidance relating to PAs exists (DH, 2011a) but a clearer understanding of the roles and numbers of PAs is required (Qureshi and McNay, 2011).

A further consequence of the practice is that the service user who employs a personal assistant becomes an employer bound by employment legislation which involves administrative responsibility of completing pay slips and tax returns and in some scenarios could lead to involvement in an employment tribunal (*Roberts v Carlin* [2010]). Guidance has been produced suggesting steps to be taken for safe recruitment of PAs by the individual (Action on Elder Abuse, no date)

Few would challenge the potential benefits of personalization for the individual: greater independence and freedom to choose and arrange care and support. There is also a concern about the potential for greater risk of abuse and exploitation (Ferguson, 2007) although ADASS warns against starting from 'an assumption that personal budgets and direct payments automatically increase risk' (ADASS and LGA, 2013:8). It is clear that safeguarding and personalization policies need to be integrated and a DH guide provides some practice examples (2010a). Individuals who choose a personal budget should still benefit from regular care plan reviews, receive advice on how to protect themselves from abuse, advice on good recruitment practice in relation to PAs and access to advocacy services.

Domiciliary services

Domiciliary services may be provided or arranged directly by the local authority or purchased with a personal budget. This represents a significant proportion of the support provided under community care assessments. It may be viewed as the traditional alternative to the appointment of a personal assistant. The CQC (2013b) identified over 4500 registered providers, providing home care to around 500,000 people. Concerns from that report are outlined in the introduction to this chapter. In addition, a report by the EHRC (2011a) voiced concern that independent home care providers (and PAs) do not have any direct duties under the Human Rights Act 1998. Although many people in their survey were satisfied with home care, they also found instances of rough handling, financial abuse, inadequate support with eating and drinking, disregard for privacy and dignity and high staff turnover, which in one case led to an elderly woman experiencing 32 different home care workers over a two-week period.

Support provisions within mental health law

Support may be provided to individuals with mental health needs. Mental health law is complex and is considered in its own volume in this series. As a prerequisite to any intervention under the Mental Health Act 1983, an individual must have a mental disorder as defined in s. 1 Mental Health Act 1983, 'any disorder or disability of the mind'.

Many responsibilities under the Act are invested in the Approved Mental Health Professional (AMHP) – a role undertaken by specially qualified social workers and other professionals (previously Approved Social Workers (ASWs)). The Act contains provisions under which individuals may be removed from their homes, or from a public place, and may be compulsorily detained in hospital (see Chapter 6). It is important to remember, however, that these compulsory measures are used in relation to a small proportion of individuals with a mental disorder. The majority of people in mental hospitals are voluntary patients and many people benefit from community mental health services.

The Mental Health Act 1983 also includes some provisions by which support may be provided to an individual with a mental disorder – this may include both individuals who experience and who perpetrate abuse.

Guardianship (s. 7) may be utilized to provide support to enable an individual to live in the community. The powers of the guardian are to stipulate where the patient lives, to require patients to attend places for medical treatment, occupation, education or training; and to have access to the patient (s. 8). In the majority of cases the local authority acts as guardian although it is possible for a private individual or organization to be appointed (Brown, 2009). Guardianship does not authorize compulsory medical treatment or deprivation of liberty.

Community treatment orders are available for patients detained under s. 3 where the patient is suitable for compulsory treatment in the community as an alternative to hospital, with the power of recall.

Aftercare is provided under s. 117 where a person has been subject to guardianship or detention for treatment. It is a jointly imposed duty on the local authority and the health authority. Aftercare must be provided until it is agreed that it is no longer required by the individual. The Act does not define aftercare services but aftercare is likely to comprise, amongst others things, social work support, domiciliary services and access to day care, residential and other facilities (*Clunis v Camden and Islington Health Authority* [1998]). Local authorities cannot charge for aftercare services (*R v Manchester City Council ex parte Stennett* [2000]). An individual has the right to refuse aftercare.

Carers

Any discussion of support and safeguarding must have regard to the role of carers. Integral to community care, carers retain a pivotal role since the advent of personalization. Without the six million or so carers, many adults would find themselves without any real alternative to residential accommodation. Carers can enable individuals to retain their independence for longer whilst enjoying a relationship. Carers were described as the first line of a preventative approach in the Coalition paper *A Vision for Adult Social Care* (DH, 2010c) and ADASS (2011) in its safeguarding advice note recognizes that: 'Carers have a range of roles regarding safeguarding: as partners and informants; themselves as vulnerable to harm and abuse; as abusers.'

Caring takes its toll. Carers UK conducted a survey of 3000 carers in 2013. Findings of concern included: 84 per cent of carers said caring had a negative effect on their health with 92 per cent saying their mental health was affected by caring; 44 per cent were in debt as a result of caring; 46 per cent had raised concerns about poor quality care services; and 15 per cent had taken a less qualified job or not taken promotion because of caring responsibilities

In a chapter on support and prevention, it is appropriate to consider the support that carers provide to vulnerable adults, but also what support is available for carers. There are three pieces of legislation which enable assessment and provision of support to carers. Some financial support is also available in the form of Carer's Allowance.

Legislation for assessment and provision of support for carers

Carers (Recognition and Services) Act 1995
Where a carer provides or intends to provide a substantial amount of care on a regular basis for a person for whom the local authority carries out a s. 47 NHSCCA 1990 assessment, the carer can request an assessment of his or her ability to provide and continue to provide care.

Carers and Disabled Children Act 2000
Carers have the right to an assessment whether or not the cared for person is being assessed. The local authority may provide 'care services' described as 'any services which the local authority sees fit to provide and will in the local authority's view help the carer care for the person cared for' (s. 2(2)).

Carer's (Equal Opportunities) Act 2004
When carrying out a s. 47 assessment, the local authority is obliged to inform the carer of his or her right to an assessment. Assessment

must include consideration of whether the carer works or wishes to work, or is undertaking or wishes to undertake any education, training or leisure activity. The local authority may request other bodies to assist it in planning provision of services, may request other bodies to provide services and, in each case, the body must give due consideration to the request.

Clements comments positively that:

> The [2004] Act marks a cultural shift in the way carers are viewed: a shift in seeing carers not so much as unpaid providers of care services for disabled people, but as people in their own right: people with the right to work, like everybody else; people who have too often been socially excluded and (like the disabled people for whom they care) often denied the life chances that are available to other people.
>
> *Clements, 2005: para. 1.4*

Nevertheless limited funds are available for carer support and there seems to be regional variation in how and how many carer assessments are carried out (Seddon, et al., 2007).

Changes to the assessment of carers' needs under the Care Act 2014 are discussed at the end of this chapter.

Carer's allowance

This is a state benefit which is payable to individuals (over 16) who spend at least 35 hours a week caring for a person who receives either Attendance Allowance or a Personal Independence Payment (the replacement for Disability Living Allowance from April 2013). Even if care is being provided to more than one person, the allowance is only payable once. It will not be paid if the individual has other income of over £100 or claims other state benefits including state pension.

Carers who work may request, but are not entitled to, flexible working if caring for an adult who is a relative, or an adult who is not a relative but lives in the same house.

On-the-spot question	Does the law relating to carers reflect the role that carers play?

Carer involvement

The role of carers has received increasing levels of recognition in the legislation cited and in policy, described as 'expert partners in care' (DH, 2010b:32). There is a clear expectation that carers will be involved in decision-making relating to the vulnerable adult, as a matter of good practice and prescribed by law: for example, in relation to best interests assessments under the MCA 2005. The following cases show that this intention may not always translate into practice and also that despite recognition of carers as experts their wishes will not always be synonymous with the best interests of the vulnerable adult.

In *G v E and Others* [2010], the court considered the role of a carer in the context of a breach of Article 8 ECHR. The carer had no involvement in a local authority decision (without approval of the Court of Protection) to remove a young man with a learning disability from the carer's home The court held that Article 8 gives 'not only substantive protection against any inappropriate interference with their family life but also procedural safeguards including the involvement of the carers in the decision-making process' [88].

In *HBCC v LG* [2010], the local authority applied for declarations regarding contact and residence arrangements for a 96-year-old woman. The court found that the woman lacked capacity to decide these matters for herself and had to determine whether it would be in her best interests to live in a care home or with her daughter. The court heard evidence of mistreatment by the daughter and that she had no real insight into her mother's care needs. It therefore ordered that she should live in a care home and have contact there with her daughter.

A further decision also concerned lack of insight by a carer into a vulnerable adult's needs. In *PCT v P and AH* (2009), the court found that the young man, who had a mild learning disability and severe epilepsy, could not decide on where he should live and what contact arrangements he should have with his adoptive mother. The court found that it was in his best interests to live in supported housing, despite his expressed wish to remain with his mother, partly because in his mother's care he was socially isolated, excluded from new experiences and prevented by his mother's over-protective carer from realizing his true potential.

> **PRACTICE FOCUS**
>
> John, 88, is cared for by his wife Ann, 78. John is almost immobile due to severe arthritis and prone to falls. He has suffered from mild depression over the years and is showing some signs of memory loss and confusion. Ann is partially hearing-disabled and waiting for a hip replacement. She finds coping for John stressful. Until recently their neighbour, Maureen, 62, also called in most days and helped with shopping. Social services visited last year at Maureen's request but could not offer any help at that time.
>
> The only toilet is downstairs. When Ann goes out shopping she locks John in the bedroom so no harm will come to him. She also makes him wear incontinence pads while she is out, though he is not incontinent. Their adult daughter Susan lives at home. She has a moderate learning disability and a physical disability. She uses a wheelchair and sleeps downstairs in the front room. Adrian, their son, visits occasionally. He has a drug and alcohol abuse problem and regularly asks for money. The last time he visited he shouted at Ann and pushed past John, knocking him over, after John refused to give him any money.
>
> - Are there any safeguarding adults concerns in this scenario?
> - What action could be taken to support this family?

Transitions and leaving care

Leaving care support

Some young adults, entitled to support from adults services, may also receive leaving care support where they have previously been in the care of the local authority. Detailed discussion of this aspect of law and practice is considered in the *Looked After Children* (Ball, 2014) and the *Children in Need of Support* (Westwood, 2014) volumes in this series. The Children Act 1989 introduced a duty to advise, assist and befriend to promote welfare when young people cease to be looked after. This was developed further in the Children (Leaving Care) Act 2000 and the Children and Young Persons Act 2008. Unaccompanied asylum seeking children are also covered by the leaving care provisions.

In outline, local authorities have responsibilities toward 16 and 17-year-olds in care, care leavers and others who were eligible before reaching 18. Each person should have a pathway plan which details information on health, education, accommodation and other matters relevant to the development of independence. Each young person should be supported by their own personal adviser whose role is to liaise with the local authority and ensure compliance with the pathway plan (*R (J) v Caerphilly County Borough Council* [2005]).

The sections on transitions in the Care Act 2014 helpfully recognize the vulnerability of young adults as they move between children's and adults' services. Sections 58–66 set out a structure for assessment of needs. A 'child's needs assessment' may be carried out when requested by a child (his or her parent or carer) to consider whether the child has needs for care and support which are likely to continue after reaching 18. Assessment of young carers and carers of children are also provided for.

Asylum seekers

General support for asylum seekers is the responsibility of the National Asylum Support Service. Limited support may be available to adult asylum seekers following *Westminster City Council v National Asylum Support Service* [2002] which confirmed that a council might be liable to provide accommodation under s. 21 National Assistance Act 1948 for needs arising from disability, not solely from destitution or its effects.

In addition to adult asylum seekers, social services have responsibilities for unaccompanied (or separated) asylum seeking children, as children in need (and consequently as children leaving care).

A major practice issue is age assessment of a young asylum seeker who may be a child. In *AS (by his Litigation Friend the Official Solicitor) v London Borough of Croydon* [2011], the court provided the following guidelines on the minimum standards for age assessment:

> (1) An appropriate adult should accompany the child and should be present during the interview.
> (2) A full and careful explanation should be given to the child of the nature of the assessment and its purpose and of the role of the assessing social worker. A careful check should be made to ensure that there is full understanding between the child and the interpreter and that the interpreter is skilled in both the language and dialect of the child and has experience of interpreting in the kind of situation created by the age assessment process.

(3) The interview should be conducted in a structured, fair, non-adversarial, non-stressful and informal manner and an informal but full note of the questions and answers should be taken by one of those present.

(4) The assessors should pay attention to the level of tiredness, trauma, bewilderment and anxiety of the child and his or her ethnicity, culture and customs should be a key focus throughout the assessment.

(5) The assessors must take a history from the child. All relevant factors should be taken into account including, but not limited to, physical appearance and behaviour. The objective is to undertake a holistic assessment.

(6) Each interview should, if practicable, be conducted by two assessors who should have received appropriate training and experience for conducting age assessment interviews on young and vulnerable children.

(7) The assessors should establish as much rapport as possible with the child (a process known as 'joining'), should ask open-ended non-leading questions using, as appropriate, circular questioning methods. The assessors should be mindful of the child having been 'coached' and that the child may have had to answer questions on relevant topics several times previously thereby unwittingly blurring the possible accuracy of the answers. Giving the child the benefit of the doubt should always be the standard practice.

(8) The assessors should give the child a fair and proper opportunity to answer any potentially adverse findings at a stage when an adverse decision is no more than provisional so as to enable him or her to provide any appropriate explanation or additional facts which might counter or modify such findings.

(9) The conclusions reached by the assessors should be explained with reasons which, although they may be brief, should explain the basis of the assessment and any significant adverse credibility or factual finding.

(10) The reasons should be internally consistent and should not exhibit any obvious error or inadequate explanation for not accepting any apparently credible and consistent answers of the child.

AS (by his Litigation Friend the Official Solicitor) v London Borough of Croydon *[2011]*

Care Act 2014 reforms

Section 1 provides that the general duty of a local authority is to promote individual well-being. Well-being is further defined and includes physical and mental health, emotional well-being and personal dignity; and protection from abuse and neglect, as well as wider aspects of well-being. The full provision is set out in Chapter 1.

Section 2 sets out the objectives for service provision, with a clear emphasis on preventing and reducing needs. This is a general duty exercisable as regards the whole population in the local authority area rather than a specific duty actionable by an individual.

s. 2

> A local authority must provide or arrange for the provision of services, facilities or resources, or take other steps, which it considers will—
> (a) contribute towards preventing or delaying the development by adults in its area of needs for care and support;
> (b) contribute towards preventing or delaying the development by carers in its area of needs for support;
> (c) reduce the needs for care and support of adults in its area;
> (d) reduce the needs for support of carers in its area.
>
> *Care Act 2014*

Section 8 is entitled 'How to meet needs' and sets out examples first of *what* might be provided (1)(a–e) and *ways* in which needs may be met in (2)(a–c).

s. 8

> (1) The following are examples of what may be provided to meet needs under sections 18 to 20—
> (a) accommodation in a care home or in premises of some other type;
> (b) care and support at home or in the community;
> (c) counselling and other types of social work;
> (d) goods and facilities;
> (e) information, advice and advocacy.
> (2) The following are examples of the ways in which a local authority may meet needs under sections 18 to 20—
> (a) by arranging for a person other than it to provide a service;
> (b) by itself providing a service;
> (c) by making direct payments.
>
> *Care Act 2014*

Assessment is covered in two sections – relating to a 'needs' assessment and a 'carers' assessment.

s. 9 Assessment of an adult's need for care and support

(1) Where it appears to a local authority that an adult may have needs for care and support, the authority must assess—
  (a) whether the adult does have needs for care and support, and
  (b) if the adult does, what those needs are. ...
(4) A needs assessment must include an assessment of—
  (a) the impact of the adult's needs for care and support on the matters specified in section 1(2),
  (b) the outcomes that the adult wishes to achieve in day-to-day life,
  (c) whether, and if so to what extent, the provision of care and support could contribute to the achievement of those outcomes, and
  (d) whether, and if so to what extent, other matters (including, in particular, the adult's own capabilities and any support available to the adult from friends, family or others) could contribute to the achievement of those outcomes.
(5) A local authority, in carrying out a needs assessment, must involve—
  (a) the adult,
  (b) any carer that the adult has, and
  (c) any person whom the adult asks the authority to involve or, where the adult lacks capacity to ask the authority to do that, any person who appears to the authority to be interested in the adult's welfare. ...

s. 10 Assessment of a carer's needs for support

(1) Where it appears to a local authority that a carer may have needs for support (whether currently or in the future), the authority must assess—
  (a) whether the carer does have needs for support (or is likely to do so in the future), and
  (b) if the carer does, what those needs are (or are likely to be in the future). ...
(3) 'Carer' means an adult who provides or intends to provide care for another adult (an 'adult needing care'); but see subsections (8) and (9). ...
(5) A carer's assessment must include an assessment of—
  (a) whether the carer is able, and is likely to continue to be able, to provide care for the adult needing care,

(b) whether the carer is willing, and is likely to continue to be willing, to do so,

(c) the impact of the carer's needs for support on the matters specified in section 1(2),

(d) the outcomes that the carer wishes to achieve in day-to-day life,

(e) whether, and if so to what extent, the provision of support could contribute to the achievement of those outcomes, and

(f) whether, and if so to what extent, other matters (including, in particular, the carer's own capabilities and any support available to the carer from friends, family or others) could contribute to the achievement of those outcomes.

(6) A local authority, in carrying out a carer's assessment, must have regard to—

(a) whether the carer works or wishes to do so, and

(b) whether the carer is participating in or wishes to participate in education, training or recreation.

(7) A local authority, in carrying out a carer's assessment, must involve—

(a) the carer, and

(b) any person whom the carer asks the authority to involve.

(8) An adult is not to be regarded as a carer if the adult provides or intends to provide care—

(a) under or by virtue of a contract, or

(b) as voluntary work.

(9) But in a case where the local authority considers that the relationship between the adult needing care and the adult providing or intending to provide care is such that it would be appropriate for the latter to be regarded as a carer, that adult is to be regarded as such (and subsection (8) is therefore to be ignored in that case).

(10) The references in this section to providing care include a reference to providing practical or emotional support.

Care Act 2014

In each case the duty to carry out the assessment applies regardless of the authority's view of the level of need for care and support, or the level of financial resources.

Each case is subject to s. 11(1) to (4) (refusal by adult of assessment).

Further reading

Carers UK (2013) *The State of Caring 2013* provides an up-to-date profile of the experience of carers.

Clements, L (2011a) *Carers and their Rights: The Law Relating to Carers* and Clements, L and C Thompson (2011) *Community Care and the Law* and are two detailed texts including commentary and analysis of the law, guidance and case law.

Davies, M (ed.) (2012) *Social Work with Adults*. Part 1 of this text is dedicated to social work and the personalization agenda and includes chapters on policy, law, theory, research and practice.

DH (2010b) *Prioritising Need in the Context of Putting People First: A Whole System Approach to Eligibility for Adult Social Care* is the current guidance on eligibility criteria.

EHRC (2011a) *Close to Home: An Inquiry into Older People and Human Rights in Home Care*: this inquiry highlights the fact that, unlike residential homes, independent homecare providers and unregulated providers such as personal assistants do not have any direct duties under the Human Rights Act 1998, yet provide the large majority of care in individuals' own homes.

Herring, J (2013) *Caring and the Law*: an excellent text which interrogates the concept of caring across the life course.

3

CRIMINAL LAW AND SAFEGUARDING

AT A GLANCE THIS CHAPTER COVERS:

- abuse as crime
- crime prevention
- the decision to prosecute
- specific offences
- special measures
- the appropriate adult
- sentencing and aggravating factors
- criminal injuries compensation

No Secrets recognizes a role for the criminal law in safeguarding:

> Some instances of abuse will constitute a criminal offence.
> In this respect vulnerable adults are entitled to the protection
> of law in the same way as any other member of the public.
> (DH, 2000b:2.8)

It is clear that some forms of abuse may constitute criminal behaviour in terms of meeting the elements of a criminal offence. Such classification inevitably means that the police will have a major role to play, alongside any other appropriate safeguarding measures. Even if an incident is not prosecuted, the police should play their part in joint investigations and can provide support and expertise in investigating cases. A properly led police interview is most likely to gather relevant and usable information in accordance with rules of evidence upon which to mount a possible prosecution. The guidance continues to explain:

Examples of actions which may constitute criminal offences are assault, whether physical or psychological, sexual assault and rape, theft, fraud or other forms of financial exploitation, and certain forms of discrimination, whether on racial or gender grounds ... Criminal investigation by the police takes priority over all other lines of enquiry.

DH, 2000b:2.8

As with other areas of law there have been developments in the criminal law, including the introduction of new offences relevant to adult abuse, since the publication of *No Secrets*. This chapter outlines the range of possible offences, organized by type of abuse, and considers the roles of key players in the criminal justice system and the ways that a victim may be supported. Not all criminal behaviour is prosecuted as such and there may be a variety of factors that influence the decision. The prosecution policy of the CPS is central to the decision once a police investigation has commenced. Other more conceptual reasons also have a bearing. Mere use of the word 'abuse' may be interpreted as implying something other than crime. It will not be appropriate for a prosecution to proceed in every case, and this may rest on questions of balancing offender management with management of victims. An appropriate focus on outcomes for the victim may favour alternative action. Against this it is clear that in some cases vulnerable adults are specifically targeted as victims of crime and pro-active use of the criminal law sends a message that society will not tolerate such behaviour. Critical awareness of the operation of the criminal justice system is necessary if, as *No Secrets* suggests, vulnerable adults are entitled to the protection of the criminal law as are other members of the public. Article 6 ECHR, the right to a fair trial, is clearly engaged in considerations as to how well a witness will present and as to the appropriate need for special measures to counter disadvantage and discrimination.

Crime prevention

Crime reduction strategies are required by the Crime and Disorder Act 1998. Section 17 states:

s. 17

> Without prejudice to any other obligation imposed upon it, it shall be the duty of each authority ... to exercise its functions with due regard to the likely effect of the exercise of those functions on, and the need to do all that it reasonably can to prevent, crime and disorder in its area.
>
> *Crime and Disorder Act 1998*

The duty is imposed on local authorities in cooperation with health, probation police and other agencies, recognizing that crime rates can be affected and reduced by various aspects of local authority functions. Examples could include the work of trading standards in raising awareness of 'doorstep fraudsters' and action by housing departments when tenants engage in anti-social behaviour.

The decision to prosecute

The CPS is the independent body responsible for prosecuting individuals charged with a criminal offence, following the gathering of evidence and investigation by the police. Increasingly, the CPS also has a role in determining whether sufficient evidence exists to charge an offence.

Central to CPS practice is the two-part test for prosecution. Firstly, there must be sufficient evidence to provide a realistic prospect of conviction and, secondly, prosecution must be in the public interest. The vulnerability of a victim, particularly if targeted because of this vulnerability, is a significant factor in assessing the public interest element. The CPS has published prosecution policy documents in relation to cases of disability hate crime (CPS, 2007) and older people (CPS, 2008). Guidance also exists in relation to 'either-way offences'. Where certain factors apply, a case may be more likely to be tried on indictment. For example, trial on indictment is preferable for cases of assault occasioning bodily harm which include violence to vulnerable people. Theft is also more likely to be tried on indictment if the victim is considered particularly vulnerable to theft.

Exercise of the choice to prosecute or not may be challenged, as in *R (B) v DPP* [2009]. A person who suffered from mental health problems had been the victim of an assault. The decision of the CPS to discontinue a prosecution on the basis that the victim was not a credible witness was irrational and involved a misapplication of the Code for Crown Prosecutors. It was also a violation of the victim's rights under Article 3 ECHR.

Prosecutions may be brought by some other bodies for defined offences. In relation to safeguarding adults, this may include the role of the CQC and of trading standards.

Specific offences

In respect of each category of abuse, a range of criminal offences may apply as considered below.

Physical abuse

A range of assault-based offences are included in the Offences Against the Person Act 1861, including assault occasioning actual bodily harm, malicious wounding, wounding with intent, and threats to kill. An additional offence, common assault, is a common law offence.

The Domestic Violence Crime and Victims Act 2004 introduced a new offence of 'causing or allowing the death of a child or vulnerable adult'. For these purposes a vulnerable adult is defined as:

s. 5(6)

> a person aged 16 or over whose ability to protect himself from
> violence, abuse or neglect is significantly impaired through physical or
> mental disability, through old age or otherwise.
> *Domestic Violence Crime and Victims Act 2004*

The Domestic Violence, Crime and Victims (Amendment) Act 2012 extends s. 5 Domestic Violence Crime and Victims Act 2004 by introducing a new offence of causing or allowing a child or vulnerable adult to suffer serious harm. 'Serious harm' in this context is equivalent to grievous bodily harm.

Sexual abuse

Relevant sexual offences are now provided under the Sexual Offences Act 2003. Key offences are rape, assault by penetration, sexual assault, engaging in sexual activity.

In relation to rape, the offence is committed by A where he intentionally penetrates the vagina, anus or mouth of another person (B) with his penis; B does not consent to the penetration; and A does not reasonably believe that B consents. Whether a belief is reasonable is to be determined having regard to all the circumstances, including any steps A has taken to ascertain whether B consents.

Consent is defined in s. 74 Sexual Offences Act 2003:

> … a person consents if he agrees by choice, and has the freedom and the capacity to make that choice.

There are also specific offences relating to adults with mental disorder which impacts on choice.

Offences against persons with a mental disorder impeding choice under the Sexual Offences Act 2003 include:

Section 30: sexual activity with a person with a mental disorder impeding choice;
Section 31: causing or inciting a person, with a mental disorder impeding choice, to engage in sexual activity;
Section 32: engaging in sexual activity in the presence of a person with a mental disorder impeding choice;
Section 33: causing a person, with a mental disorder impeding choice, to watch a sexual act.

Looking more closely at the elements of the offence of sexual activity with a person with a mental disorder impeding choice, s. 30 provides:

s. 30

(1) A person (A) commits an offence if—
    (a) he intentionally touches another person (B),
    (b) the touching is sexual,
    (c) B is unable to refuse because of or for a reason related to a mental disorder, and

(d) A knows or could reasonably be expected to know that B has a mental disorder and that because of it or for a reason related to it B is likely to be unable to refuse.

(2) B is unable to refuse if—

  (a) he lacks the capacity to choose whether to agree to the touching (whether because he lacks sufficient understanding of the nature or reasonably foreseeable consequences of what is being done, or for any other reason), or

  (b) he is unable to communicate such a choice to A.

Sexual Offences Act 2003

Further offences exist which focus on circumstances where sexual abuse occurs in violation of the special relationship a care worker has. The 'care worker' offences are:

> **Section 38:** care workers: sexual activity with a person with a mental disorder;
>
> **Section 39:** care workers: causing or inciting sexual activity with a person with a mental disorder;
>
> **Section 40:** care workers: sexual activity in the presence of a person with a mental disorder;
>
> **Section 41:** care workers: causing a person with a mental disorder to watch a sexual act;
>
> **Section 38:** care workers: sexual activity with a person with a mental disorder.

There is a presumption that a care worker (within s. 42) will know that the individual has a mental disorder.

Section 42 defines care workers (A) for these purposes:

s. 42

  (a) B is accommodated and cared for in a care home, community home, voluntary home or children's home, and

  (b) A has functions to perform in the home in the course of employment which have brought him or are likely to bring him into regular face to face contact with B.

(3) This subsection applies if B is a patient for whom services are provided—

  (a) by a National Health Service body or an independent medical agency;

  (b) in an independent hospital; or

  (c) in Wales, in an independent clinic,

and A has functions to perform for the body or agency or in the hospital or clinic in the course of employment which have brought A or are likely to bring A into regular face to face contact with B

(4) This subsection applies if A—

    (a) is, whether or not in the course of employment, a provider of care, assistance or services to B in connection with B's mental disorder, and

    (b) as such, has had or is likely to have regular face to face contact with B.

Sexual Offences Act 2003

A person who is convicted of an offence contained in ss 30–41 involving a victim with a mental disorder will automatically be included on the barred list provided under the Safeguarding Vulnerable Groups Act 2006 (SVGA 2006) (discussed further in Chapter 5)

Psychological abuse

It would be unusual for a person who suffers physical or sexual abuse, for which the offences discussed above may be charged, without there also being an element of psychological suffering and which would be relevant for sentencing in considering the impact of the offence on the victim. Additionally, there are some specific offences applicable to scenarios of psychological abuse alone.

Instances of harassment fall within the Protection from Harassment Act 1997. Under s. 2 a person must not pursue a course of conduct which amounts to harassment of another, and which he or she knows or ought to know amounts to harassment of the other. Harassment includes alarming the person or causing the person distress (s. 7), speech is included as 'conduct' and a 'course of conduct' must include at least two incidents. The Act was introduced following a number of high-profile stalking cases, but the offence is broader than that and would include bullying, name-calling and anti-social behaviour targeted at an individual.

Related offences include putting a person in fear of violence under s. 4 Protection from Harassment Act 1997 which would apply where a person has suffered harassment and fears violence will be used against him or her (and the defendant knew or ought to know that his or her behaviour would cause that fear). Finally, the Criminal Justice and Police Act 2001 contains the offence of harassment of a person in his or her home (s. 42A).

Ill-treatment and neglect

Section 44 MCA 2005 provides a new offence of ill-treatment or neglect:

s. 44

(1) Subsection (2) applies if a person ('D')—
   (a) Has the care of a person ('P') who lacks, or whom D reasonably believes to lack, capacity,
   (b) Is the donee of a lasting power of attorney, or an enduring power of attorney (within the meaning of Schedule 4), created by P, or
   (c) Is a deputy appointed by the court for P.
(2) D is guilty of an offence if he ill-treats or wilfully neglects P.
(3) A person guilty of an offence under this section is liable—
   (a) On summary conviction, to imprisonment for a term not exceeding 12 months or a fine not exceeding the statutory maximum or both;
   (b) On conviction on indictment, to imprisonment for a term not exceeding 5 years or a fine or both.

MCA 2005

The Code of Practice confirms that ill-treatment and wilful neglect are separate offences (Department for Constitutional Affairs (DCA), 2007). In either case it is necessary to show that the victim of the offence lacks or is reasonably believed to lack capacity. As previously stated, capacity is issue-specific under the MCA 2005 and a question arises as to what issue capacity is assessed for under this section. The Court of Appeal suggests capacity relates to the care of the person when the offence is committed, but that is rather vague and seems inconsistent with the approach of the MCA 2005 (*R v Dunn* [2010], followed in *R v Hopkins and Priest* [2011]). The offence can be committed in any setting, although research suggests many prosecutions relate to abuse in care homes (Brammer, 2014).

A similar offence, s. 127 Mental Health Act 1983, ill-treatment of patients, provides:

s. 127

(1) It shall be an offence for any person who is an officer on the staff of or otherwise employed in, or who is one of the managers of, a hospital, independent hospital or care home—
   (a) to ill-treat or wilfully to neglect a patient for the time being receiving treatment for mental disorder as an in-patient in that hospital or home; or

(b) to ill-treat or wilfully to neglect, on the premises of which the hospital or home forms part, a patient for the time being receiving such treatment there as an out-patient.

(2) It shall be an offence for any individual to ill-treat or wilfully to neglect a mentally disordered patient who is for the time being subject to his guardianship under this Act or otherwise in his custody or care (whether by virtue of any legal or moral obligation or otherwise).

Mental Health Act 1983

This offence applies to individuals being treated for mental disorder in particular settings. The issue of capacity is not relevant.

Former staff at Winterbourne view were convicted of this offence (McGregor, 2012).

On-the-spot question	What factors might influence the CPS to prosecute under s. 44 MCA 2005 rather than an assault-based charge where the ill-treatment is a physical attack?

Financial abuse

Theft may range from small amounts of change taken by an individual collecting an older person's pension to multi-million pound organized crime. The case of *R v Hinks* [2000] provides an example. John Dolphin, a 53-year-old man described as being of limited intelligence, was befriended by Hinks, a 38-year-old woman. The sum of £60,000 was given to Ms Hinks over eight months and she was found guilty of theft. Herring (2013) argues that this is a just conviction given the context of the relationship.

Where elderly people are specifically targeted for burglary this will be taken into account as a significant aggravating factor. Examples include *R v Cawley* [2008], where a sentence of eight years was upheld for burglary of a man in his nineties, by a persistent offender. It was irrelevant that the wallet which was taken was soon recovered. Burglary may be accompanied with physical violence, as in *R v Passoni* [2010], in which the 77-year-old victim was punched by an 18-year-old several times before he stole from her.

The separate offence of fraud is contained in s. 1 Fraud Act 2006 and punishable with a maximum sentence of 10 years (either way). Confidence fraud may feature in some of the cases where trading standards are involved, e.g. in circumstances where a rogue trader falsely tells a victim that expensive repairs are required to the victim's roof and takes the money having carried out no work or poor work.

Other offences relating to breaches of registration of care homes and offences under the SVGA 2006 are discussed in Chapter 5.

The trial

At the trial, proceedings follow a standard procedure and for a conviction the court (magistrates or judge and jury) must be satisfied 'beyond reasonable doubt' of the defendant's guilt. There are provisions for additional support at the trial for certain individuals.

Special measures

The Youth Justice and Criminal Evidence Act 1999 introduced a range of 'special measures' which are designed to enable vulnerable and intimidated witnesses to give their best evidence to the court. The Act is supported by guidance, *Achieving Best Evidence in Criminal Proceedings: Guidance on Interviewing Victims and Witnesses, and Guidance on Using Special Measures* (2011).

Eligibility for special measures depends on a witness falling within the definition of a vulnerable witness in s. 16, as a person suffering from mental disorder or otherwise having a significant impairment of intelligence and social functioning, or a physical disorder or disability, or an intimidated witness defined in s. 17 as a person suffering from fear or distress in relation to testifying (automatically includes witnesses in sexual offences cases).

Special measures

Section 23: screening the witness from the defendant;
Section 24: giving evidence via live link;
Section 25: removal of wigs and gowns during testimony;
Section 26: giving evidence in private in intimidation cases;
Section 27: video-recording of evidence in chief;
Section 28: video-recording of cross-examination and re-examination;
Section 29: examination through an intermediary;
Section 30: provision of aids for communication, e.g. sign and symbol boards (*R v Watts (James Michael)* [2010]).

R v Cox [2012] EWCA Crim 549

An intermediary may be appointed by the court to assist where the witness has difficulty communicating (see discussion by Plotnikoff and Woolfson, 2008). The function of an intermediary is to communicate to the witness questions put to the witness and to any person asking such questions the answers given by the witness in reply to them and to explain such questions or answers so far as necessary to enable them to be understood by the witness or person in question.

Cox, was a 26-year-old man with complex learning difficulties. He was convicted of the rape of a 20-year-old woman, whom he had known for some time, after an evening out drinking together. The Court of Appeal had to decide whether he had experienced a fair trial in the absence of the assistance of a registered intermediary.

Provision of an intermediary is a discretionary measure and the trial judge has overall responsibility to ensure the trial proceeds fairly with effective participation of the defendant. In this case it was not possible, despite best efforts, to secure the service of an intermediary. In the circumstances the judge adopted other measures, described in the judgment:

> These included short periods of evidence, followed by twenty minute breaks to enable the appellant to relax and his coun-sel to summarize the evidence for him and to take further instructions. The evidence would be adduced by means of very simply phrased questions. Witnesses would be asked to express their answers in short sentences. The tape-recordings of the interview should be played, partly to accustom the jury to the appellant's patterns of speech, and also to give the clearest possible indication of his defence to the charge. For this purpose it was an agreed fact before the jury that 'Anthony Cox has complex learning difficulties. He could understand simple language and pay attention for short peri-ods'. [21]

The judge concluded that the interests of justice required him to maintain a close control over the questioning, to intervene where any possible unfairness might arise, and to ensure that the appellant was not unduly stressed by the proceedings. He would have to be 'rather more interventionalist' than normal. He would play 'part of the role which an intermediary, if available, would otherwise have played'. He recognized the continuing obligation on him to monitor his 'initial conclusion' on these issues. He plainly did so. [22]

The Court of Appeal found that these modifications were sufficient to ensure a fair trial and the appeal was dismissed.

If the witness has become physically or mentally unfit by the time of the trial the police statement may be read out and admitted as hearsay evidence (s. 116(2) Criminal Justice Act 2003).

Vulnerable witnesses may also benefit from wider support measures including Victim Support, the Witness Service and provisions within the Code of Practice for Victims of Crime (MoJ, 2013) issued under the Domestic Violence Crime and Victims Act 2004. Support and preparation of witnesses must not, however, step into the realms of witness training (*R v Momodu* [2005]).

Whether or not the witness is assisted by the provision of special measures, there is a basic requirement that the witness is competent to give evidence i.e. he or she can understand questions put to him or her and can give answers to them which can be understood (s. 53 Youth Justice and Criminal Evidence Act 1999). This operates as a presumption, thus it would be necessary to prove that the person lacked competence.

In *R v D* [2002] admissibility of evidence was challenged. The defendant appealed against the admissibility of video testimony of his alleged victim (B) in a trial for sexual offences. B was an 81-year-old woman who had been diagnosed as being in the early stages of Alzheimer's disease. The defendant argued that B was not a competent witness at the time of the video testimony and her evidence should be ruled inadmissible. It was found that in deciding whether to admit the video testimony the judge had applied a sound test, namely whether the witness had seemed to understand the questions being put to her and whether she had given answers which could be understood. On that basis the evidence was admissible.

Evidence

Detailed coverage of rules of evidence are beyond the scope of this text (for a full explanation see Cooper (2014) in this series).

Key elements of the law on evidence include the requirement for evidence to be: relevant; first-hand rather than hearsay evidence is preferred; and experts may give opinion evidence within their area of expertise. There are some differences between rules of evidence in criminal and civil cases, however, the points above would also be relevant in Court of Protection proceedings, another significant jurisdiction for safeguarding adults cases where capacity of the individual is impaired.

The requirement for a fair hearing is reinforced by Article 6 ECHR. A violation of Article 6 was found in the case of *R (King) v Isleworth Crown Court* [2001]. The judge stated: 'This case raises points of some interest, both in relation to the treatment by the courts of people with disabilities and also in relation to the increased emphasis on fairness which has accompanied the coming into force of the Human Rights Act 1998.'. King appeared as a self-represented litigant. He waited from 10am until 4pm for his case to be heard, by which time he was extremely tired and stressed. He argued successfully that the judge had failed to make allowances for the impact a stroke had on his ability to conduct the hearing. Also, the court had not followed advice in the *Equal Treatment Bench Book* (Judicial College, 2013) regarding persons with disabilities, which notes the possible need for more time and that the stress of coming to court may exacerbate symptoms.

The appropriate adult

Vulnerable suspects have some support in the criminal process, largely through the role of the **appropriate adult** and some access to special measures, though this is more limited than discussed above for witnesses/victims.

Authority for the provision of appropriate adults is the Police and Criminal Evidence Act 1984, specifically *Code C: The Code of Practice for the Detention, Treatment and Questioning of Persons by Police Officers* (2012). As it will not always be clear to police officers whether the suspect is mentally vulnerable, the Code states:

> If an officer has any suspicion, or is told in good faith, that a person of any age may be mentally disordered or otherwise mentally vulnerable, in the absence of clear evidence to dispel that suspicion, the person shall be treated as such for the purposes of this Code.
>
> *Police and Criminal Evidence Act 1984, Code C: para 1.4*

The role of the appropriate adult is described as:

they shall be informed:

- that they are not expected to act simply as an observer; and
- that the purpose of their presence is to: advise the person being interviewed; observe whether the interview is being conducted properly and fairly; and facilitate communication with the person being interviewed.

Police and Criminal Evidence Act 1984, Code C: para. 11.16

An appropriate adult for a person who is mentally disordered or learning disabled may be one of the following:

- a relative, guardian or other person responsible for care or custody;
- someone who has experience of dealing with mentally disordered or mentally handicapped people but is not a police officer or employed by the police; or
- some other responsible adult who is not a police officer or employed by the police (Police and Criminal Evidence Act 1984, *Code C*: Annex E, para. 2).

Social workers are clearly included within the second category and the custody officer at the police station may contact social services and ask the authority to provide an appropriate adult (White, 2002). An appropriate adult must be present if the vulnerable adult is charged or cautioned.

In addition, under s. 77 Police and Criminal Evidence Act 1984 a jury must be warned about the reliability of a confession by a person with a learning disability.

Sentencing

The Criminal Justice Act 2003 provides the current framework for sentencing and identifies four purposes of sentencing: punishment; reduction of crime; reform and rehabilitation; protection of the public and reparation by offenders. In arriving at a decision on sentence the court has some discretion within the maximum specified penalty, but sentencing guidelines exist and provide a structured approach to consideration of the seriousness of the offence, any aggravation factors and mitigation.

Aggravated versions of some offences exist in which the maximum penalty for an offence is increased where it is racially or religiously aggravated. For example, assault occasioning actual bodily harm normally carries a maximum penalty of five years but where aggravated this is increased to seven years. The Legal Aid, Sentencing and Punishment of Offenders Act 2012 adds transgender identity to the personal characteristics which are statutory aggravating factors in sentencing when an offence is motivated by hostility to the victim. Beyond these statutory examples, offences may be aggravated and sentence increased if the victim is vulnerable and if targeted because of their vulnerability and if the offence takes place in a domestic setting.

Criminal injuries compensation

Where a crime has taken place, the Criminal Injuries Compensation Scheme (Ministry of Justice (MoJ), 2012) provides a tariff compensation scheme. An adult who has suffered abuse may qualify for compensation. The requirements (set out in detail in the scheme documentation) are principally twofold. First, the incident which gave rise to the injury must be reported to the police as soon as practicable (there is some discretion to take account of age and capacity). It is not necessary for a prosecution to follow. Secondly, the scheme relates to crimes of violence which are defined in Annex B as follows:

a physical attack;
b any other act or omission of a violent nature which causes physical injury to a person;
c a threat against a person causing fear of immediate violence in circumstances which would cause a person of reasonable firmness to be put in such fear;
d a sexual assault to which a person did not in fact consent; or
e arson or fire-raising.

Many instances of sexual and physical abuse would be covered. Claims are determined by a claims officer and there is a procedure for review and subsequent appeal relating to the determination of a claim.

The scheme includes a tariff for injuries with a section on the 'Physical abuse of adults including domestic abuse', and recognizes that a person may sustain a number of injuries as part of a pattern of abuse. By way of example, the payment for serious abuse described as 'intermittent physical assault resulting in an accumulation of healed wounds burns or scalds, but with no appreciable disfigurement' is £2000. For a 'persistent pattern of severe abuse over a period of more than 3 years', this rises to £8200.

The scheme recognizes that sexual offences may result in physical injury and/or mental illness and the tariff includes a specific section for sexual offences where the victim is an adult 'who by reason of mental illness is incapable of giving consent'.

It would be reasonable for a social worker to draw the scheme to the attention of an adult who has suffered abuse that fits the 'crime of violence' criteria and assist with completion of the claims form.

PRACTICE FOCUS

Susan is 31 and lives with her parents, John and Ann. She has a moderate learning disability and uses a wheelchair. She attends a day centre three days each week. A gang of youths have been calling her names and following her home. They have started throwing objects at her, a stone caused a large graze to her arm, and have threatened to attack her parents while she is out. Susan has told her parents she doesn't want to go to the day centre anymore but won't tell them why.

- Has an offence been committed here?
- If so, do you think a prosecution is likely?

Further reading

Brown (2012) and EHRC (2011) include consideration of particular crimes. CPS (2008), Home Office (1999) and NPIA (2011) are relevant guidance.

Brown, H (2012) 'Not only a crime but a tragedy […] exploring the murder of adults with disabilities by their parents' 14(1) *Journal of Adult Protection* 6

CPS (2008) *Prosecuting Crimes Against Older People*

EHRC (2011) *Hidden in Plain Sight: Inquiry into Disability-related Harassment*

Home Office (1999) *Caring for Young People and the Vulnerable? Guidance for Preventing Abuse of Trust*

NPIA (2011) *Guidance on Safeguarding and Investigating the Abuse of Vulnerable Adults*

4

CAPACITY AND SAFEGUARDING

AT A GLANCE THIS CHAPTER COVERS:

- the Mental Capacity Act 2005 and Code of Practice
- assessing capacity
- key principles
- best interests
- decision-making where an individual lacks capacity
- lasting powers of attorney and deputyship
- the Court of Protection
- Deprivation of Liberty Safeguards
- the Independent Mental Capacity Advocate

In safeguarding work a key question will be whether the victim of abuse has capacity to make their own decisions. Generally speaking, where an adult has capacity and can be described as free to make autonomous decisions, the law will not interfere in the absence of any criminal behaviour. For safeguarding cases where the adult may lack capacity, the MCA 2005 is relevant.

A significant number of people will experience some lack of capacity during their lifetime and inevitably some of those individuals will experience abuse. It may also be the case that some people with impaired capacity will be particularly vulnerable to abuse. In part that may be due to location. Around 80 per cent of care home residents have dementia or severe memory problems and will be affected by many of the MCA 2005's provisions, including for some, the DOLS (Alzheimer's Society, 2013).

The key sources of law here are the MCA 2005, the Code of Practice (DCA, 2007) and a developing body of case law. The Act applies to anyone aged over 16 who lacks capacity to make a decision. For those aged 16–18 relevant provisions of the Children Act 1989 would also apply. The Code includes a specific chapter (14) relevant to safeguarding entitled 'What means of protection exist for people who lack capacity to make decisions for themselves?', however, it is necessary to have a good understanding of the whole of the Act.

The Code of Practice

The MCA 2005 is supported by a Code of Practice which provides explanation and detailed guidance on the operation of the Act (DCA, 2007). A separate code on the DOLS (MoJ, 2008, discussed below) was issued with the introduction of those provisions. The MCA 2005 Code is intended to be useful and accessible to everyone who might be involved with someone who lacks capacity. In addition, certain people have a duty to have regard to the MCA 2005 Code when acting in relation to a person who lacks capacity or whose capacity is being assessed (s. 42). This includes:

- people working in a professional capacity, such as, social workers, care managers, doctors, paramedics, nurses;
- people being paid to provide care or support, such as care assistants, providers of domiciliary services;

- the donee of an LPA and a **deputy**;
- an IMCA.

If relevant to proceedings, a court (civil, criminal or tribunal) will take into account any failure to comply with the MCA 2005 Code.

The Code is an important document and anyone working in this field needs to be familiar with it. *R (Munjaz) v Mersey Care NHS Trust* [2005] was a case in which the status of the Code of Practice to the Mental Health Act 1983 was considered. The House of Lords found that, although the Code of Practice to the Mental Health Act provided guidance and not instructions, a hospital had to consider it with great care and depart from it only if it had cogent reasons for doing so. The same priority is likely to be given to the MCA 2005 Code.

Assessing capacity

Individuals may lack capacity to make decisions due to a range of factors including learning disability, brain injury, the effect of drugs or alcohol, dementia and other mental health problems. The MCA 2005 includes a key definition at s. 2 of incapacity.

s. 2

(1) a person lacks capacity in relation to a matter if at the material time he is unable to make a decision for himself in relation to the matter because of an impairment of, or a disturbance in the functioning of, the mind or brain.
(2) It does not matter whether the impairment or disturbance is permanent or temporary …
(3) A lack of capacity cannot be established merely by reference to—
    (a) person's age or appearance, or
    (b) a condition of his, or an aspect of his behaviour, which might lead others to make unjustified assumptions about his capacity.

MCA 2005

The provision refers to 'a matter' at 'the material time' indicating at the outset that capacity is assessed in relation to a particular decision at the time the decision needs to be made – there is no room for global assessments of incapacity (*Masterman Lister v Brutton & Co, Jewell & Home Counties Dairies* [2002]).

There is both a diagnostic and a functional element to the definition. First, it will be necessary to establish that the person has an 'impairment of, or a disturbance in the functioning of the mind or brain'. Second, as a result, the person is 'unable to make a decision'. The term 'unable to make a decision' is further defined in s. 3. Subsection (2) recognizes that in many cases impairment or disturbance in the mind or brain will not be a permanent state of affairs but a person so affected no matter how temporarily, e.g. due to the influence of drugs, may nevertheless be incapacitated. Subsection (3) adds an important steer against making unjustified assumptions based on stereotypes or born out of discriminatory judgments. Clearly, not all people who are elderly lack capacity and equally it would be wrong to assume that a person with a manifest physical disability, e.g. cerebral palsy, lacked capacity.

Being unable to make a decision is central to the definition of incapacity.

s. 3

(3) A person is unable to make decision for himself if he is unable—
  (a) to understand the information relevant to the decision
  (b) to retain that information
  (c) to use or weigh the information as part of the process of making the decision, or
  (d) to communicate his decision (talking, sign language, other means).
                                                                    MCA 2005

Two further points are relevant to the assessment. Explanations of relevant information must be given in an appropriate way, which may include for example, the use of visual aids (s. 3(2)). The MCA 2005 also states that it is only necessary to retain information for a short period (s. 3(3)), recognizing fluctuating capacity. Case law has further developed understanding of the test.

The information referred to is information about the reasonably foreseeable consequences of deciding one way or another, or failing to make the decision (s. 3(4)). This point was considered in *A Local Authority v Mrs A and Mr A* [2010]. The local authority had removed two children from Mr and Mrs A at birth and, concerned that she might become pregnant again, applied for a declaration that Mrs A lacks capacity to decide whether to use contraception. The local authority submitted that capacity to decide included awareness of what is involved in caring for a child. In the view of the judge that set the bar too high. Instead, the court was to consider if Mrs A had the 'ability to understand and weigh up the immediate medical issues surrounding contraceptive treatment (the proximate medical issues)'. That included the reason for contraception and what it does, which includes the likelihood of pregnancy if it is not used; the types available and how each is used; the advantages and disadvantages of each; the possible side effects of each and how they can be dealt with; how easily each type can be changed; and the generally accepted effectiveness of each.

A further case concerning capacity to consent to sexual relations demonstrates the commitment of the court to encouraging participation and decision-making by the individual. In *D Borough Council v B* [2011] the local authority sought a declaration that Alan, described as a 41-year-old man with a moderate learning difficulty and vigorous sex drive, lacked capacity to consent to sexual relations. Mostyn J stated that:

> capacity to consent to sex remains act-specific and requires an understanding and awareness of: the mechanics of the act; that there are health risks involved particularly the acquisition of ... sexually transmissible infections; and that sex between a man and a woman may result in the woman becoming pregnant.
> (*D Borough Council v B* [2011] [42])

The court found that Alan did not have capacity but made an interim declaration and ordered the local authority to provide Alan with sex education, in the hope that he could gain that capacity, to be reviewed in nine months.

A further decision, which considered factor s. 3(3)(c) was prompted by a local authority application to the Court of Protection for a declaration authorizing force-feeding of a woman with anorexia nervosa. In *Re E* [2012] J Jackson found that:

> there is strong evidence that E's obsessive fear of weight gain makes her incapable of weighing the advantages and disadvantages of eating in any meaningful way. The need not to gain weight overpowers all other thoughts. [49]

Who will assess capacity?

In *RT v LT and a Local Authority* [2010] (see p. 83) a consultant psychiatrist gave expert evidence to the court on the assessment of capacity. That is not typical of the vast majority of capacity assessments, however: a criticism of multi-agency work involving mental capacity is that many practitioners are still unclear who completes capacity assessments and who

> **KEY CASE ANALYSIS**

RT v LT and A Local Authority [2010]

In *RT v LT and A Local Authority* [2010], the Court of Protection had to decide whether a young woman with mild learning disabilities and mental health problems had capacity to decide where to live and with whom to have contact. The court applied the test in s. 2(1) MCA 2005 and found that the woman was 'unable to make a decision', focusing on her inability to use or weigh information, as she had very fixed ideas on certain topics. An expert, Dr K, consultant psychiatrist, provided an opinion to the court, noting the difficulty LT had in using information as part of the decision-making process. The judgment states:

> In his assessment of LT's capacity he noted particular difficulties in LT making balanced judgments, as she was only able to look at a problem from one perspective. The nature of her social disorder ... limited her ability to take in and weigh the relevant information and, in extreme circumstances, communicate it effectively. Thus he concluded, she demonstrated strong dichotomous (black and white) thinking: for example, social workers were all bad and only lie; parents were all good and never had any problem. [25]

The case also confirmed that:

> the individual incapacities set out in section 3(1) are not cumulative. A person lacks capacity if any one of the subsections a to d applies. In the instant case I am satisfied that s. 3(1)(c) applies. [2010] [40]

determines best interests (SCIE, 2011). It is important to remember that there is scope under the MCA 2005 structure for a variety of professionals and lay people to assess capacity, for example, social workers, psychologists, dentists, occupational therapists, housing officers, lawyers etc. Exactly who will depend on the particular decision to be made. In relation to safeguarding cases, social workers will often be required to conduct an assessment of capacity (McDonald, 2010). Carers, whether paid or provided by an agency or family members or relatives, will also frequently make assessments of capacity to make a particular decision. Unlike cases falling under the Mental Health Act 1983 which require a psychiatric opinion:

> Provided there is credible expert evidence upon which the court can be satisfied that the individual concerned lacks capacity that, in our judgment is sufficient. It would be simply unreal to require psychiatric evidence in every case, quite apart from the fact that it would in some cases be irrelevant. To require such evidence would in our judgment make MCA 2005 unworkable.
>
> G v E *[2010]*

There are some circumstances when a professional will need to be involved in an assessment. The MCA 2005 Code provides examples, including: where there is disagreement among family members about a person's capacity; where there is a conflict of interest between the assessor and person being assessed; where somebody has been accused of abusing an adult who may lack capacity to make decisions to protect themselves; and where the person being assessed expresses different views to different people (4.53). A formal assessment may be legally required in cases including: where a person's capacity to sign a legal document could be legally challenged; if a decision about a person's capacity is required in legal proceedings and to establish whether a person might need to be assisted by the **Official Solicitor**; and where there may be legal consequences of a finding of capacity, e.g. determining a compensation claim (4.54).

Ultimately where the question of capacity is disputed it must be determined to the civil standard of proof – balance of probabilities (s. 2(4) MCA 2005). In practice it may be necessary to take action before the question can be finally determined, in that case the court has ruled that there must 'simply be sufficient evidence to justify a reasonable belief that P may lack capacity in the relevant regard' (*Re F (by her Litigation Friend)* [2010]).

Principles

The MCA 2005 starts with five key principles which apply to all aspects of capacity and decision-making:

- a person must be assumed to have capacity unless it is established that he or she lacks capacity (s. 1(2));
- a person is not to be treated as unable to make a decision unless all practicable steps to help him or her to do so have been taken without success (s. 1(3));

- a person is not to be treated as unable to make a decision merely because he or she makes an unwise decision (s. 1(4));
- an act done, or decision made, under this Act for or on behalf of a person who lacks capacity must be done, or made, in his or her best interests (s. 1(5));
- before the act is done, or the decision is made, regard must be had to whether the purpose for which it is needed can be as effectively achieved in a way that is less restrictive of the person's rights and freedom of action (s. 1(6)).

The principles apply to day-to-day practice as much as they do to the operation and decision-making of the Court of Protection.

There is much emphasis in the MCA 2005 on enabling and encouraging the individual to make as many decisions for him or herself as possible. Social workers have a key role here in utilizing skills to promote empowerment. This commitment applies even if an individual does not have capacity to make the actual decision. In that case, s. 4(4) MCA 2005 provides further that the person making the determination (as to what is in a person's best interests):

s. 4

(4) ... must so far as reasonably practicable, permit and encourage the person to participate, or to improve his ability to participate, as fully as possible in any act done for him and any decision affecting him.

MCA 2005

On-the-spot question	Reflect on different ways of encouraging participation in decision-making where a person may lack capacity and any resources that you might need.

Best interests

An act done, or decision made, under this Act for or on behalf of a person who lacks capacity must be done, or made, in his or her best interests (s. 1(5) MCA 2005). All relevant circumstances must be considered when arriving at a best interests decision. The Act also directs consideration of specific factors in a checklist in s. 4:

- whether the person might regain or develop capacity to make the decision in the future and when;

- the ascertainable past and present wishes and feelings of the person concerned (including any relevant written statements);
- the beliefs and values that would be likely to influence the person's decision if he or she had capacity (including religious beliefs and cultural values);
- other factors the individual would be likely to consider if able to do so (this might include a sense of family obligation);
- the views of others it is considered appropriate to consult including anyone so named, carers and others interested in the person's welfare and any donees of an LPA or deputies appointed under the Act.

Additional factors will often be relevant. Records should be kept of how best interests decisions are arrived at, including details of individuals consulted.

It may seem obvious to state that best interests decisions must be person-centred. In *AH v Hertfordshire Partnership NHS Foundation Trust* [2011], an application of policy would have meant A moving from a specialist residential service in the grounds of a long-stay hospital, where he had lived for many years, to urban supported housing. The judge commented: 'Guideline policies cannot be treated as universal solutions, nor should initiatives designed to personalise care and promotion of choice be applied to the opposite effect.' [74]–[80]

The case of *ITW v Z and Others* [2009] illustrates the application of the best interests criteria in a structured way. Munby J stated that in applying the best interests criteria there is no hierarchy of factors beyond the overarching principle of what is in P's best interests; the weight of factors will differ in each case and there may be one or more factors of 'magnetic importance' to the particular case. He then focused on the aspect of P's wishes and feelings as follows:

i) First, P's wishes and feelings will always be a significant factor to which the court must pay close regard,
ii) Secondly, the weight to be attached to P's wishes and feelings will always be case-specific and fact-specific,
iii) Thirdly, in considering the weight and importance to be attached to P's wishes and feelings the court must of course, ... have regard to *all* the relevant circumstances. In this context the relevant circumstances will include, ...
   a) The degree of P's incapacity, for the nearer to the borderline the more weight must in principle be attached to P's wishes and feelings;

b) The strength and consistency of the views being expressed by P;

c) The possible impact on P of knowledge that her wishes and feelings are not being given effect to;

d) The extent to which P's wishes and feelings are, or are not, rational, sensible, responsible and pragmatically capable of sensible implementation in the particular circumstances; and

e) Crucially, the extent to which P's wishes and feelings, if given effect to, can properly be accommodated within the court's overall assessment of what is in her best interests.

ITW v Z and Others *[2009] [35]*

The court will often adopt a 'balance sheet' approach to best interests decisions. This was evident in *G v E* [2010], *An NHS Trust v K* [2012] and *Dorset County Council v EH* [2009].

In the *Dorset* case, Parker J set out a checklist of 'benefits and burdens' outlined in the table below. The council had applied for a declaration that it was lawful for an 82-year-old woman with Alzheimer's to reside in a residential home and for reasonable and proportionate force to be used to transport her there and prevent her leaving. The council was concerned about risks to her if she remained in her home environment:

Benefits of staying at home: – keep habits developed over years, carry on with limited independence – not depressed – does not feel unsafe	**Risks of staying at home:** – not eating/drinking – out-of-date/rotten food – insufficient/irregular medication – poor personal hygiene, skin care, clothing – wandering – risk of accidents, fire – psychological distress at night
Benefits of moving: – regular meals – prompting with self-care – help from staff – warm clothing – reassurance at night – relationships with other residents? – physical safety – risks eliminated – less strain on brother – anti-dementia medication	**Risks of moving:** – loss of independence – short-term risk of anger and distress – long-term risk of depression – 'giving up' – less opportunity to walk – sociability risks

Table 4.1: Checklist of benefits and burdens

Decision-making when an individual lacks capacity

Where an individual is assessed as lacking capacity for a particular decision or act, the MCA 2005 provides options and legal protection for those who act on their behalf. This may be via a broad permission under s. 5, 'Acts in connection with care or treatment', or formal appointment of individuals to take those decisions in the adult's best interests via LPAs or deputyship.

Some decisions are excluded from the MCA 2005. They cannot be made on behalf of a person by the Court of Protection, a deputy or attorney or under s. 5. Excluded decisions are listed in s. 27 and include consenting to marriage, civil partnership, divorce or dissolution, sexual relations and the adoption of a child. The court may intervene where this rule is abused, e.g. if a person enters into a marriage contract though lacking capacity to do so. The court can also rule on whether the person does in fact have capacity for the particular decision as, in relation to marriage, in *Sheffield City Council v E and S* [2004] and, more recently, *A, B, C v X and Z* [2012].

'Acts in connection with care or treatment'

Section 5 states: 'It is lawful for any person to do an act when providing care for another person if he believes the person lacks capacity in relation to the matter and it is in his best interests.'

This is intended to be a positive permission giving provision. Actions will only be protected from **liability** if it is reasonably believed that the person being cared for lacks capacity. Some assessment of capacity and best interests must therefore precede the action. Many day-to-day decisions and acts by carers and by social workers will be covered by this section and accurate recording is essential. There are limits to the powers provided under s. 5:

- the protection offered by s. 5 does not extend to any negligent acts, i.e. where the duty of care is breached by a particular action or failure to act;
- s. 5 will not protect decisions which override valid advance refusals of treatment;
- s. 5 does not authorize any act or decision which conflicts with a decision made by a donee of an LPA or a deputy.

In *R (Sessay) v South London and Maudsley NHS Foundation Trust* [2011], the court considered the police removal of a woman suffering from a mental disorder from domestic premises to a hospital. The police purported to remove the woman using the authority of s. 5. The court held that the police were mistaken in this practice and had acted unlawfully in removing the woman from her home to the hospital. They should have used the specific powers under the Mental Health Act 1983, contained in s. 136 (removal from a public place) and s. 135 (removal with a warrant from domestic premises).

Section 5 may permit restraint (use of force or restriction of liberty) but only if two conditions are met: it is necessary to prevent harm to P; and it is a proportionate response to the likelihood and seriousness of harm. Section 5 will not authorize a deprivation of liberty – see discussion of DOLS below.

Lasting powers of attorney

Any person (over 18) with capacity may execute an LPA appointing an attorney to make decisions on his or her behalf in the event of loss of capacity. The detail for this new order, which replaces the enduring power of attorney, is contained in ss 9–14 MCA 2005. There are two types of LPA – personal welfare and property and affairs, which provide a high level of flexibility for the individual who wishes to plan ahead. The attorney cannot act on a matter where the donor has capacity.

To take effect the LPA must be registered with the Public Guardian. As a safeguard there is a requirement for a 'prescribed person' to certify that the donor understands the nature of the LPA and was not under any pressure to sign the document. The Public Guardian maintains a register of LPAs. Should any disputes arise it is appropriate to report to the Office of the Public Guardian (OPG) and ultimately the Court of Protection has jurisdiction. An attorney appointment may be revoked, as in *Re Harcourt; The Public Guardian v A* [2013]. A son was appointed as an attorney to act in relation to his mother's property and affairs. The local authority raised concerns with the OPG and it found that the attorney had sold his mother's house and bought another property in his sole name together with a vehicle, totalling £146,000.

Deputyship

A deputy/deputies may be appointed by the Court of Protection where there is an ongoing need for decisions to be made regarding welfare and/or financial matters (s. 16). Ordinary day-to-day decisions would remain covered as s. 5 MCA 2005 acts, but a deputy may be required if, for example, there were regular complex medical or financial decisions to be made or in situations of regular conflicts between the opinions of family members themselves or with other professionals as to the best interests of the individual.

The deputy must be reliable, trustworthy and competent and must consent to the appointment – it cannot be imposed. A local authority may be appointed, as in *R (M) v Birmingham City Council* [2008]. In other circumstances, a professional deputy such as a solicitor or a family member, may be the most suitable option. *Re P* [2010] suggested that there will often be a family preference. Subsequently, *Re M; N v O and P* [2013] outlined a general order of preference, namely: spouse or partner; other relative with a personal interest in P's affairs; close friend; professional adviser; local authority representative; and panel deputy. The deputy will be supervised by the Public Guardian and the court may revoke the appointment, or vary the deputy's powers, if he or she contravenes his or her authority or behaves in a way that is not in the person's best interests. Even where a deputy has specific powers, if the individual has capacity in relation to that matter the deputy cannot act (s. 20(1)). There are some limits on the powers of a deputy. A deputy cannot restrict contact with the person, as in *Re SK (Vulnerable Adult: Capacity)* [2008]; cannot execute a will on his or her behalf; and cannot do anything which is inconsistent with an LPA.

The Court of Protection

The MCA 2005 established a new specialist court with jurisdiction to determine any disputes relating to capacity. The court has a central office but may sit anywhere in England and Wales. Half of all hearings are taking place in regional courts (Judiciary of England and Wales, 2011).

The court has powers to make declarations: as to whether X lacks capacity for Y decision; personal welfare decisions such as where to live; contact; consent to treatment or surgery; and property and affairs decisions, such as to manage property, execute a will or conduct proceedings. For example, in *An NHS Trust v DE and Others* [2013], the court ordered that it would be in the best interests of a man with profound learning difficulties to have a vasectomy as this would permit him greater independence; and in *Westminster City Council v C* [2008] the court made an order preventing a man with severe learning disabilities from being taken out of the country for a proposed marriage.

In relation to deprivation of liberty, the court provides an appeal mechanism and can terminate authorizations or vary conditions. If a deprivation of liberty is sought in a venue other than a care home or hospital, this can only be authorized by the court. Where there are disputes about LPAs, the court can rule on objections to LPAs and determine validity.

Declarations may be made on an interim (*SMBC v WMP* (2011)) and final basis. Where ongoing decision-making is required, the court can appoint a deputy/deputies to make personal welfare, property and affairs decisions. A decision by the court is preferred to the appointment of deputy.

The court may request reports from the Public Guardian, Court of Protection Visitor (*A v A Local Authority* [2011]), local authority and NHS body. The Official Solicitor will usually act for the person who lacks capacity.

The MCA 2005 Code suggests the following circumstances when it would be appropriate to involve the court:

- there is genuine doubt or disagreement about the existence, validity or applicability of an advance decision to refuse treatment;
- there is a major disagreement regarding a serious decision (for example, about where a person who lacks capacity to decide for themselves should live);
- a family carer or a solicitor asks for personal information about someone who lacks capacity to consent to that information being revealed (for example, where there have been allegations of abuse of a person living in a care home);
- someone suspects that a person who lacks capacity to make decisions to protect themselves is at risk of harm or abuse from a named individual (the court could stop that individual contacting the person who lacks capacity) (DCA, 2007:8.28);
- consideration of certain medical treatments including withholding or withdrawing artificial nutrition and hydration from a patient in a persistent vegetative state, organ or bone marrow donation by a person who lacks capacity;
- non-therapeutic sterilization (*A Local Authority v K and Others* [2013]);
- cases where there is doubt about whether the proposed treatment is in the person's best interests (DCA, 2007: 8.18);

- cases where disputes between healthcare staff and family cannot be resolved (DCA, 2007: 8.23).

Who can apply to the Court of Protection?

Applications to court may be made by a variety of people, depending on the particular circumstances, including the person whose capacity is in issue. For example, local authorities may make applications about where a person is to live; NHS trusts may make applications about serious medical treatment. Those with a right to apply are: the person who lacks or is alleged to lack capacity, the donor of an LPA, an attorney, a deputy, or a person named in an existing court order. Others require leave of the court and when deciding this the court will consider:

s. 50(3)

    (a) the applicant's connection with the person to whom the application relates,
    (b) the reasons for the application,
    (c) the benefit to the person ... of a proposed order or directions, and
    (d) whether the benefit can be achieved in any other way.

MCA 2005

Publicity

The relevant law is contained in the Court of Protection Rules 90–93. Under r. 90 it is a general rule that Court of Protection hearings are to be held in private. The rules include a list of people who are entitled to attend a private hearing, including the parties and their legal representatives. Where an application is made for an order allowing some form of publicity or media attendance, a two-stage test applies.

First there must be 'good reason' to make the order, and even if good reason is shown, the court has a discretion to exercise. Secondly, the court must decide, having balanced the Article 8 and Article 10 ECHR claims, if the order is justified, and on that basis may still restrict publicity even if initial good reason appears.

The court allowed some form of publicity in the following cases (amongst others): *W (by her Litigation Friend, B) v M* [2011]; *Hillingdon London Borough Council v Neary* [2011]; *G v E and Others* [2010] and *A v Independent News & Media Ltd* [2010]. Reasons for allowing some publicity included the fact that information was already in the public domain, that it is in the public interest to have some understanding of the jurisdiction and to provide accountability for poor practice. The court will balance competing claims under Articles 8 and 10 ECHR and even if a case is heard in open court it may impose reporting restrictions against revealing the identity of the parties (Brammer, 2012). Recent practice guidance has extended the circumstances when permission will be given for suitably anonymized judgments to be published (Munby, 2014).

Enforcing orders of the court

The use of contempt orders have been considered in Court of Protection proceedings and a particular case, *SCC v LM and Others* [2013], attracted a high level of media interest. Following this decision, new Practice Directions on 'Committal for contempt of court' have been issued ([2013] EWHC B7 (COP) and [2013] EWHC B4 (COP)). It is clear that in appropriate cases contempt will be used to ensure compliance with the order of the court.

The Public Guardian

The Public Guardian maintains the register of LPAs and manages the work of deputies. The role is supported by the work of the Court of Protection Visitor who may investigate cases on behalf of the Public Guardian. Where concerns are raised about the actions of a deputy or attorney, under s. 58 MCA 2005 the Public Guardian must investigate (Hartley-Jones, 2011). The Public Guardian role is explained further in the OPG's *Safeguarding Policy* (2013).

The Court of Protection Visitor

Section 61 provides for the appointment of Court of Protection Visitors. In carrying out their function, visitors are entitled to examine and take copies of health records, local authority records and care home records relating to the person. The visitor may also interview the person in private.

Deprivation of Liberty Safeguards

The DOLS were introduced by the Mental Health Act 2007 into the MCA 2005. A separate Code of Practice document was published to support the new area of law (MoJ, 2008). A person subject to DOLS is referred to as a detained resident, i.e. someone detained in a hospital or care home for the purpose of being given care and treatment, in circumstances which amount to a deprivation of liberty.

The safeguards were introduced following the decision in *HL v UK* [2004] in which detention of an individual unable to give his consent was found to be in breach of Article 5(1) ECHR (right to liberty and security of the person) and Article 5(4) ECHR (right to speedy review of detention). The lack of a procedure in law to authorize HL's deprivation of liberty was commonly referred to as the 'Bournewood gap', the intention behind the introduction of DOLS being to fill that gap. The safeguards should ensure that, where a deprivation of liberty is contemplated, approval is sought and will only be granted where the deprivation is in the best interests of the person. A route to challenge the deprivation is then in place, together with other safeguards for the individual. Nevertheless, it is arguable that in some cases use of DOLS in itself may be abusive rather than providing a safeguard, for example, see the case of *Neary* below. It would also appear that some people are subject to restrictions in care homes and hospitals without the protection of DOLS. The law, procedures and application process for DOLS are quite complex and, even in its most recent report, the CQC (2013) notes that levels of awareness and understanding of the DOLS system appear low amongst relevant practitioners.

The CQC monitors the operation of DOLS in England and produces an annual report. The CQC should be notified directly of all DOLS applications and their outcomes. The number of applications and number of granted authorizations has increased each year since the introduction of DOLS in 2009. Concerns remain, however, that rates of application and granted authorizations vary quite significantly by region (CQC, 2013). The HSCIC (2013) found 14.1 applications per 100,000 in London and 48.6 per 100,000 in East Midlands. The largest proportion of applications are for older adults with dementia in care homes, but DOLS can apply to anyone to whom the MCA 2005 applies, including, for example, younger adults with brain injury.

As a matter of good practice, prior to any application for DOLS, effort should be made to maximize the individual's freedom, reduce the need for deprivation of the individual's liberty and to ensure that any necessary restriction is minimized.

Managing authority

Care homes and hospitals are **managing authorities** and have responsibility for applying to **supervisory bodies** for a DOLS authorization. It is possible for the managing authority to grant itself an urgent authorization for up to seven days (extendable in exceptional circumstances for a further seven days), whilst an application for a standard authorization is being considered.

Supervisory body/authority

The supervisory body receives the DOLS application, commissions six assessments and decides whether or not to grant the authorization. If granted, the supervisory body can stipulate the length of the authorization and impose conditions. A standard authorization can be granted for up to 12 months.

Since April 2013 local authorities have taken on all supervisory body responsibilities, (they were previously shared by local authorities and primary care trusts). Some supervisory body staff are located within the local authority safeguarding team. In order to avoid potential conflict it is essential that there are clear, accountable arrangements for keeping a separation between the areas of work.

The supervisory body appoints a representative for the person (relevant person's representative (RPR)). This may be a member of the person's family or, in some circumstances, an IMCA may be appointed under s. 39(d).

The six assessments

1 **Age:** the person must be 18 or over.
2 **Mental health:** the person must have a mental disorder as defined under the Mental Health Act 1983.
3 **Mental capacity:** the person must lack capacity to make the decision to be accommodated in the hospital or care home and deprived of liberty.
4 **Best interests:** it must be in the person's best interests to be a detained resident to prevent harm to themselves and the deprivation is a proportionate response to the likelihood and seriousness of harm for them to be a detained resident.
5 **Eligibility:** the person is not subject to Mental Health Act compulsion including guardianship and community treatment orders.
6 **No refusals:** the authorization must not conflict with any valid refusal to the decision from a deputy or under an LPA.

If all six conditions are met an authorization may be made.

There may be occasions where an individual could receive care and treatment either under the MCA 2005 and DOLS framework or under the Mental Health Act 1983 regime. The case of *South London and Maudsley NHS Foundation Trust v Secretary of State for Health* [2013] suggests that the least intrusive legal framework should apply and, in most cases, this will be the MCA 2005 regime.

Reviews and referrals to the Court of Protection

There is a review process available to the managing authority and supervisory body and the individual or their representative can ask the supervisory body to review an authorization and carry out new assessments.

It is also possible to bring a challenge to the authorization in the Court of Protection. The Court may determine questions relating to: whether the qualifying requirements were met (often focusing on best interests, see *Re M* [2013]); the purpose of the authorization; conditions; and the period of the authorization.

A wealth of case law on DOLS has developed (selection below) and should be read in conjunction with the law and the Code of Practice (MoJ, 2008). The greatest challenge for the courts and practitioners has been in clarifying the difference between a restriction of liberty and a deprivation of liberty (Cairns et al., 2011; Hewitt, 2012). Examples of deprivations include high levels of supervision, physical restraints, preventing an individual having access to relatives, keeping the person locked in and forcibly giving medication.

> → **KEY CASE ANALYSIS** ←

DOLS case law

JE v DE and Surrey County Council [2006]: a 76-year-old man was taken from the care of his wife because of a risk of harm and neglect to live in a care home. He consistently expressed the wish to return to his wife but was not permitted to leave the care home. The circumstances amounted to a deprivation of liberty.

P (otherwise known as MIG) and Q (otherwise known as MEG) v Surrey County Council [2011]: The Court of Appeal decided that two sisters with learning disabilities were living in arrangements in their best interests which did not amount to a deprivation of liberty. MIG lived with a foster carer and went to further education. If she had attempted to leave the foster home by herself she would have been restrained from doing so. Her sister lived in a secure residential home.

She received tranquilizing medication for anxiety and was sometimes physically restrained. She also attended college.

Hillingdon London Borough Council v Neary [2011]: Steven Neary, a 20-year-old man with autism and a learning disability, lived with his father. His father agreed that he should go into temporary residential accommodation for respite following a period of illness. He was retained in the accommodation for his best interests despite the father's opposition and his own expressed wishes to return to his father. The local authority was criticized on a number of levels. The initial detention before a DOLS authorization was unlawful, the subsequent authorizations were flawed, an IMCA had not been appointed and there was a breach of Article 8 ECHR (the right to respect for private and family life).

Cheshire West and Chester Council v P [2011]: the Court of Appeal found no deprivation of liberty in a case concerning a 38-year-old man living in supported housing who lacked capacity to make decisions regarding residence and care. He needed a high level of care and wore a bodysuit sewn up the front to prevent him removing and ingesting his continence pads. Munby LJ introduced the notion of a 'relevant comparator', i.e. a person with similar needs not an ordinary adult. He also referred to the need to consider objective and subjective reasons for a placement.

P (by his Litigation Friend the Official Solicitor) v Cheshire West and Chester Council and Another; P and Q (by their Litigation Friend the Official Solicitor) v Surrey County Council [2014]: The Supreme Court judgment in the conjoined appeal of Cheshire West and P and Q (MIG and MEG) clarifies the meaning of deprivation of liberty. An objective standard will be applied, namely, a person is subject to a deprivation of liberty if he or she is under continuous supervision and not free to leave. The 'relative normality' interpretation was rejected by Lady Hale in the lead judgment, explaining that being deprived of liberty 'must be the same for everyone, whether or not they have physical or mental disabilities', and 'If it would be a deprivation of my liberty to be obliged to live in a particular place, subject to constant monitoring and control, only allowed out with close supervision, and unable to move away without permission even if such an opportunity became available, then it must also be a deprivation of the liberty of a disabled person. The fact that my living arrangements are comfortable, and indeed make my life as enjoyable as it could possibly be, should make no difference. A gilded cage is still a cage.' [46]

The decision adds much needed clarity and authorizations are likely to increase significantly as a result. Further change may follow, however, as the House of Lords Select Committee on the MCA 2005 reported that the DOLS are not fit for purpose and should be replaced with legislation that is in keeping with the language and ethics of the MCA 2005 as a whole.

On-the-spot question   On reflection, do DOLS provide an effective means of promoting human rights?

The Independent Mental Capacity Advocate

The MCA 2005 introduced an additional safeguard for certain people who lack capacity to make certain decisions – the IMCA. The object of the IMCA service is that:

s. 35(4)

a person to whom a proposed act or decision relates should, so far as practicable, be represented and supported by a person who is independent of any person who will be responsible for the act or decision.

MCA 2005

An IMCA will be made available to a person who lacks capacity to make a serious decision and has no family or friends (or deputy/LPA) to consult about a serious decision (ss 37–38 MCA 2005). A 'serious decision' means a decision about serious medical treatment or a decision about moving to long-term accommodation. An IMCA will be instructed by the local authority for decisions about moves into long-term accommodation (or change of accommodation) having carried out an assessment of the person under the National Health Service and Community Care Act 1990 and decided the move may be necessary. If an NHS body proposes the move, e.g. from hospital to a nursing home, it will instruct an IMCA. If a change of accommodation is required urgently, it may proceed but an IMCA must be appointed as soon as possible afterwards.

The IMCA remit was subsequently extended to have a role in relation to deprivation of liberty, care reviews and also in an adult protection case, even where the adult has people he or she could consult. The local authority has a discretion to involve an IMCA in a safeguarding case where it is thought likely to benefit the individual. Research conducted in the first 12 months of IMCA involvement in adult safeguarding found that in 57 per cent of cases the alleged perpetrator was a family member (Redley et al., 2011). The same research also found that safeguarding cases tended to be much more complex than the other situations where IMCAs are statutorily required to be involved and might include a number of decisions. Nevertheless, Williams et al. (2013) report that the IMCA service is underused in cases of elder abuse.

Local authorities need to have clear procedures in place for instructing an IMCA. The MCA 2005 Code advises:

The responsible body should also have procedures, training and awareness programmes to make sure that:

- all relevant staff know when they need to instruct an IMCA and are able to do so promptly
- all relevant staff know how to get in touch with the IMCA service and know the procedure for instructing an IMCA
- they record an IMCA's involvement in a case and any information the IMCA provides to help decision-making
- they also record how a decision-maker has taken into account the IMCA's report and information as part of the process of working out the person's best interests (this should include reasons for disagreeing with that advice, if relevant)
- they give access to relevant records when requested by an IMCA under section 35(6)(b) of the Act
- the IMCA gets information about changes that may affect the support and representation the IMCA provides
- decision-makers let all relevant people know when an IMCA is working on a person's case,
- and decision-makers inform the IMCA of the final decision taken and the reason for it.

DCA, 2007:10.14

Examples are given of possible scenarios when it might not be practical or appropriate to consult family or friends and an IMCA would need to be instructed:

> ... an elderly person with dementia may have an adult child who now lives in Australia, or an older person may have relatives who

very rarely visit. Or, a family member may simply refuse to be consulted. (DCA, 2007:10.77)

As ever, an important practice step is to record the decision to instruct an IMCA and the reasoning behind it.

The role of the IMCA is to: provide support to enable the person to participate in the decision; follow the principles of the MCA 2005; obtain and evaluate relevant information, e.g. medical reports, social care assessments; ascertain what the person's wishes and feelings would be and his or her beliefs and values; ascertain and consider alternative courses of action; obtain further medical opinion if required, and the views of professionals working with the individual; and produce a report which must be taken into account when a decision is made. The IMCA has the power to interview the person privately, examine and copy relevant records, including health, social services and care home records and challenge the decision-maker. The MCA (Independent Mental Capacity Advocates) (General) Regulations 2006 provide more detail on the IMCA role.

PRACTICE FOCUS

Unfortunately John's health has deteriorated further and following a stroke and a diagnosis of the onset of dementia he is provided with a room in a nursing home. He has not settled well and becomes quite agitated at times. He has expressed a wish to return home but the nursing home has taken the view that this would not be appropriate and he spends most of his time in his room, which is only accessible with a keypad. One mealtime he lashes out at a staff member who is serving his lunch. He breaks a drinking glass which cuts his hand. He is initially restrained, then given a mild sedative in order for his hand to be attended to.

Ann visits the next day and is very concerned about John. She asks if she can take John into the garden but is told that could only happen if a member of staff accompanies them. John becomes very upset when Ann leaves and the home manager suggests Ann should only visit once a week until he settles. Ann would like John to come home but doesn't feel able to care for his increased levels of need.

• How does the MCA 2005 apply to this scenario?

Further reading

Ashton DJ, G (2012) *Mental Capacity: Law and Practice*: an authoritative text on the Act, written by a judge of the Court of Protection and including a copy of the Act and copies of the Codes.

DCA (2007) *Mental Capacity Act 2005 Code of Practice*

Johns, R (2014) *Capacity and Autonomy*: this text in the Focus on Social Work Law series considers capacity and autonomy throughout the life course.

McDonald, A (2010) 'The impact of the 2005 Mental Capacity Act on social workers' decision making and approaches to the assessment of risk' 40 *British Journal of Social Work* 1229: this article and Redley et al. (2010) below are two useful articles considering the roles of social workers and IMCAs under the MCA 2005.

MoJ (2008) *Deprivation of Liberty Safeguards: Code of Practice to Supplement the Mental Capacity Act 2005 Code of Practice*

Redley, M, I C H Clare, L Luke and A J Holland (2010) 'Mental Capacity Act (England and Wales) 2005: the emergent Independent Mental Capacity Advocate (IMCA) service' 40(6) *British Journal of Social Work* 1812

5

REGULATION

AT A GLANCE THIS CHAPTER COVERS:

- regulation of individuals – the Safeguarding Vulnerable Groups Act 2006
- professional regulation – the Health and Care Professions Council
- the role of the Care Quality Commission
- regulation of residential accommodation
- whistleblowing

Appropriate regulation of the workforce and of relevant settings is an important aspect of prevention and measure of accountability. The law has developed mechanisms designed to prevent unsuitable people from working with vulnerable adults (and children) and to reinforce good recruitment practices. Nevertheless, there remain some unregulated areas as identified in Chapter 2 regarding PAs. The CQC holds responsibility for the inspection and regulation of adult care services. The work of the regulator and its relationship with safeguarding teams has a vital role in safeguarding practice, although concerns have been expressed about a 'lack of clarity about responsibilities' (CSCI, 2008:16). Despite the existence of a regulatory body, it seems that awareness of abuse is often reliant on the actions of whistleblowers. The chapter therefore includes discussion of the scheme of employment protection for whistleblowers together with the campaigning work of Public Concern at Work (PCAW).

Safeguarding Vulnerable Groups Act 2006

The idea of a list of people unsuitable to work with vulnerable adults whom prospective employers could check was first introduced by the Care Standards Act 2000 as the Protection of Vulnerable Adults Index applicable across adult social care. Some aspects of the scheme were problematic with the procedures for provisional listing of care workers found to be in breach of Articles 6(1) and 8 ECHR (*R (Wright and Others) v Secretary of State for Health and Another* [2009]). A new vetting and barring scheme was introduced by the SVGA 2006, replacing the Protection of Vulnerable Adults (POVA) scheme.

The vetting and barring scheme has been further amended by the Protection of Freedoms Act 2012. The functions of the Independent Safeguarding Authority (established under the SVGA 2006) have been integrated with the functions of the Criminal Records Bureau into a new organization, the **Disclosure and Barring Service** (DBS). The emphasis of the DBS continues to be on ensuring that only suitable people continue to work or volunteer with children and vulnerable adults and it establishes both a barred list for adults and a barred list for children. As previously, a person may be included on just one or both lists. A person listed on the barred list who engages or seeks to engage in a regulated activity commits a criminal offence. Also, organizations have a duty to ensure that they do not knowingly engage a barred person in a regulated activity. Although one of the objectives of the changes introduced by the Protection of Freedoms Act 2012 was to simplify the system, it remains quite complex. A number of key definitions feature in the scheme.

s. 60

> A vulnerable adult is defined as a person aged 18 or more to whom an activity which is a regulated activity relating to vulnerable adults ... is provided.
>
> *SVGA 2006*

The original definition of regulated activity was amended by the Protection of Freedoms Act 2012 and is now set out in the SVGA 2006 as follows:

Regulated activity

(a) the provision to an adult of health care by, or under the direction or supervision of, a health care professional (all health care including physical or mental health and palliative care and first aid),

(b) the provision to an adult of relevant personal care (personal care means physical assistance, given to a person who needs it by reason of age, illness or disability, in connection with: eating or drinking; toileting; washing or bathing; dressing; oral, skin, hair or nail care; required prompting and supervision of the above; training, instruction, advice or guidance relating to the above).

(c) the provision by a social care worker of relevant social work to an adult who is a client or potential client,

(d) the provision of assistance in relation to general household matters to an adult who is in need of it by reason of age, illness or disability (general household matters include day to day managing of a person's cash, paying bills and shopping),

(e) any relevant assistance in the conduct of an adult's own affairs (by a LPA, EPA, IMHA, IMCA, independent advocacy services),

(f) the conveying by persons of a prescribed description in such circumstances as may be prescribed of adults who need to be conveyed by reason of age, illness or disability,

(g) such other prescribed activities involving, or connected with, the provision of health care or relevant personal care to adults.

Schedule 4 SVGA 2006: para. 7

Entry on the barred list.

An individual's name may be placed on the barred list:

- automatically when an offence under ss 30–41 Sexual Offences Act 2003 has been committed;
- where certain other offences have been committed (e.g. rape, murder, ill-treatment or wilful neglect, other sexual offences) and the person has been or might in future be engaged in regulated activity – the individual may make representations as to why he or she should not be included on the list;
- where he or she has engaged in relevant conduct including conduct which endangers (or is likely to) a vulnerable adult, inappropriate conduct involving sexually explicit images of violence, inappropriate conduct of a sexual nature involving a vulnerable adult and he or she is or has been or may in future be engaged in regulated activity;
- where it appears that a person may harm, cause to be harmed, put at risk of harm, attempt to harm or incite another to harm a vulnerable adult and he or she is or has been or may in future be engaged in regulated activity.

A person will be barred for a minimum period of one, five or ten years depending on their age at the time of inclusion. Review of their inclusion may be considered by the DBS and the person may be removed from the list if it is not appropriate for him or her to be included because of a change of circumstances, or if information has come to light which was not available at the time of inclusion, or error. Appeals may be made to the Upper Tribunal against a decision to include or refusal to remove a person from the list.

Under the new scheme there is provision for a criminal record certificate to be sent to the applicant to allow possible challenge of the information prior to disclosure. The applicant will also be able to request an independent review of whether information is relevant for disclosure. An Update Service has been introduced which enables a person who subscribes to the service to take their certificate with them from one role or job to another. The Update Service keeps the certificate up to date and avoids the need for multiple applications for new certificates.

Each case will be considered on its own facts as the following examples (decided under the POVA scheme) illustrate.

In *SK v Secretary of State for Health* [2011], following emergency cancellation of registration of the residential home that she managed, SK's name was added to the POVA list as unsuitable to work with vulnerable adults. Concerns included: shouting at service users and members of staff; failure to promote independence of residents and buying clothes with service users' money without their involvement; using a service user's money to buy furniture; threatening and dismissing staff if they complained to the regulatory body; and failing to carry out appropriate recruitment checks for new staff.

In *Salisu v Secretary of State for Health* [2011], S was convicted of wilful neglect of a patient contrary to s. 127 Mental Health Act 1983. S was responsible for implementing the care regime for the patient which included 24-hour one-to-one care. The patient was left unsupervised for a period leading up to his death. The conviction was clear evidence of misconduct which harmed, or placed at risk of harm, a vulnerable adult. However, the tribunal noted his good work record, that this was a single act and in its view, as there was no prospect of reoccurrence of this type of misconduct, he was not considered unsuitable to work with vulnerable adults and his name was removed from the POVA list.

Professional regulation

Social work is the focus of this book, hence the major discussion of professional regulation relates to social work and social care regulation. It is important to note, however, that there are professional bodies with similar regulatory functions acting in respect of other professional groups with a role in safeguarding. Examples include the Nursing and Midwifery Council and the General Medical Council. There are also specific bodies to deal with complaints against members of certain professions, such as the Independent Police Complaints Commission (IPCC) and the Solicitors Regulation Authority.

The Care Standards Act 2000 created the General Social Care Council (GSCC) as the regulatory body for social work. The legislation also established a professional register and made it an offence for a person not registered as a social worker to use the title of social worker (s. 61). The Health and Social Care Act 2012 abolished the GSCC. The Health and Care Professions Council (HCPC) took over responsibility for regulation of social work from the GSCC in 2012 and holds the professional register. Alongside social workers, the HCPC has responsibility for regulation of a range of health professionals including dieticians, chiropodists, occupational therapists, physiotherapists, paramedics and speech therapists (among others).

The HCPC can suspend individuals, add conditions to their practice or remove the individual from the register, meaning that he or she can no longer practice as a social worker. The forum for such decisions is a fitness to practise hearing before a panel. The professional practice of a social worker is judged against the *Standards of Proficiency: Social Workers in England* (HCPC, 2012) (linked to the *Professional Capabilities Framework* (PCF) (The College of Social Work, 2012) and the *Standard of Conduct, Performance and Ethics* (HCPC, 2008)). The former is specific to social workers as a threshold standard for entry into the profession. The latter applies to all professional groups registered with the HCPC. The key headings from each document are set out below. More detail is provided via subheadings in the full documents.

The *Standards of Proficiency: Social Workers in England* (HCPC, 2012) require that social workers:

1 'be able to practise safely and effectively within their scope of practice';
2 'be able to practise within the legal and ethical boundaries of their profession';
3 'be able to maintain fitness to practise';
4 'be able to practise as an autonomous professional, exercising their own professional judgement';
5 'be aware of the impact of culture, equality and diversity on practice';
6 'be able to practise in a non-discriminatory manner';
7 'be able to maintain confidentiality';
8 'be able to communicate effectively';
9 'be able to work appropriately with others';
10 'be able to maintain records appropriately';
11 'be able to reflect on and review practice';
12 'be able to assure the quality of their practice';
13 'understand the key concepts of the knowledge base relevant to their profession';
14 'be able to draw on appropriate knowledge and skills to inform practice';
15 'be able to establish and maintain a safe practice environment'.

The *Standards of Conduct, Performance and Ethics* (HCPC, 2008) set out these duties as registrant:

1 You must act in the best interests of service users.
2 You must respect the confidentiality of service users.
3 You must keep high standards of personal conduct.
4 You must provide (to us and any other relevant regulators) any important information about your conduct and competence.
5 You must keep your professional knowledge and skills up to date.
6 You must act within the limits of your knowledge, skills and experience and, if necessary, refer the matter to another practitioner.
7 You must communicate properly and effectively with service users and other practitioners.
8 You must effectively supervise tasks that you have asked other people to carry out.
9 You must get informed consent to provide care or services (so far as possible).
10 You must keep accurate records.
11 You must deal fairly and safely with the risks of infection.
12 You must limit your work or stop practising if your performance or judgement is affected by your health.
13 You must behave with honesty and integrity and make sure that your behaviour does not damage the public's confidence in you or your profession.
14 You must make sure that any advertising you do is accurate.

Research by McLaughlin (2010) considered decisions of the Care Standards Tribunal where social workers appealed (to the Care Standards Tribunal) against misconduct findings by the regulatory body, at that time the GSCC. In each case the social worker had either been refused registration by the Registration Committee or had been removed from the Register by the Conduct Committee. The Conduct Committee applies the civil standard of proof, 'balance of probabilities', and the onus is on the social worker to prove their suitability to practise. Some cases concerned questions of whether qualifications obtained elsewhere met the requirements of UK professional training and registration. Other cases concerned aspects of behaviour including disclosure of health information, criminal convictions and employment records. A significant proportion of the cases (40 per cent) concerned social workers who had inappropriate relationships with service users.

In *Brownbill v GSCC (Interim Suspension of Registration)* [2012], a social worker received a police caution for growing cannabis at her home for her own use. She appealed against a two-year suspension of registration imposed by the Conduct Committee. On appeal the tribunal took account of remorse shown, as indicated in her statement:

> In reflecting upon the possible causal effects of my actions and the Conduct Committee's criticism of me I do feel very genuinely remorseful that any public knowledge of my criminal actions may have brought my profession into disrepute and even made some individual social workers' tasks more difficult by reducing their credibility, or their ability to confront service users whose parenting is poor due to drug use. I have a very genuine respect for my colleagues and am extremely regretful if an already difficult task has been made more difficult with some groups of service users. The public knowledge of my criminal actions may not affect younger children but I am very aware that adolescents and adults could use my actions to justify their own illegal drug use. [18]
>
> Brownbill v GSCC (Interim Suspension of Registration) *[2012]*

The tribunal substituted a six-month suspension.

In *Ford v GSCC* [2011] a social worker was suspended after extreme pornography was found on his home computer. Suspension of registration for 18 months was considered too severe in *Boodhoo v GSCC* [2011] for making private calls on a mobile phone supplied by her employer. Removal from the register was a proportionate sanction in *Senyange v HCPC* [2012], a case of dishonesty where a social worker had made false claims for child care allowances resulting in an overpayment of over £23,000. She also failed to disclose the conviction to her employer and missed child protection visits to service users whilst attending court. In *Alanson v GSCC* [2011] application for registration to the GSCC was refused in a case where a social worker had made persistent unwanted advances to a colleague and failed to maintain appropriate professional boundaries with a service user including kissing on the mouth. The Conduct Committee of the Care Council for Wales that initially dealt with the complaint had allowed registration to continue subject to an admonishment.

Regulation of services

Accountability for good service provision, which meets the needs of service users and minimizes the risk of abuse, lies with a number of bodies. Local authorities may directly provide some services but have an increasingly important role in commissioning services from the private and not-for-profit sector. It is permissible to create contracts which require standards of care above the minimum levels stipulated by law (discussed below), but never to contract out of such minimum requirements.

The Human Rights Act 1998 will apply to providers where under s. 6 they are deemed to be 'carrying out functions of a public nature'. This

---

> **KEY CASE ANALYSIS**

YL v Birmingham City Council [2007]

In *YL v Birmingham City Council* [2007], the House of Lords decided 3:2 that when providing accommodation and care under a local authority contract independent sector care providers were not carrying out a public function – merely providing a service under a private contractual arrangement – and were therefore not public authorities for the purposes of the Human Rights Act 1998. Accordingly, these providers are not required by the Human Rights Act 1998 to act compatibly with the ECHR rights.

Section 145 Health and Social Care Act 2008 reverses this position. It ensures that the protections provided by the Human Rights Act 1998 apply to people receiving publicly arranged care in an independent sector care home by defining a person providing care in a care home as exercising a function of a public nature in doing so. It does not, however, extend to all contracted-out services, such as domiciliary care, or to self-funded residents who make their own arrangements, or people placed in care homes as 'aftercare services' under s. 117 Mental Health Act 1983.

Section 145 states:

A person who provides accommodation, together with nursing or personal care, in a care home for an individual under arrangements made with P under the relevant statutory provisions is to be taken for the purposes of subsection (3)(b) of section 6 of the Human Rights Act 1998 to be exercising a function of a public nature in doing so.

As such, an action could now be brought against a home owner under s. 7 claiming failure to protect residents' rights under the ECHR.

proved to be a contentious notion in a series of cases regarding residential accommodation and resulted in a change to the law. The National Assistance Act 1948 provides the central duty on local authorities to provide residential accommodation for those 'in need of care and attention not otherwise available to them' where ordinarily resident in the local authority area. The same residential accommodation may provide care for individuals whose care is financed by the local authority and for individuals who are self-funding.

Regulation and inspection of services has been addressed via legislation in the form of the Registered Homes Act 1984, the Care Standards Act 2000 and currently the Health and Social Care Act 2008, with key supporting regulations, the Health and Social Care Act 2008 (Regulated Activities) Regulations 2010 (the 2010 Regulations) and the Care Quality Commission (Registration) Regulations 2009.

The focus of the remainder of this chapter is on residential care, however, much of the law applies equally to other services such as domiciliary care.

The Care Quality Commission

The roles of the Healthcare Commission, Mental Health Act Commission and the CSCI were combined to form one body, the CQC, under the Health and Social Care Act 2008. The CSCI had responsibility for regulation and inspection of residential accommodation and other services prior to the CQC.

The role of the CQC is set out in the Health and Social Care Act 2008 and supporting regulations – essentially it is responsible for registration and inspection of providers of health and social care and enforcement of the regulations. The core legal framework is provided by the Act and the regulations provide detail on the expectations for good quality care. The main objective of the CQC, set out in s. 3 Health and Social Care Act 2008, is to promote the health, safety and welfare of people who use health and social care services. The CQC has a *Safeguarding Protocol* (2013c) which describes its role in safeguarding both children and adults across health and social care sectors.

The owner (and manager if applicable) of a service providing a regulated activity must be registered with the CQC. It is an offence not to be registered. Registration may be granted subject to certain conditions, can be suspended and also cancelled on specific grounds. The requirement is for the person to be fit to be a registered manager, which entails being of good character, physically and mentally fit to carry on the regulated activity and with the necessary qualifications, skills and experience (reg. 6, 2010 Regulations)

Powers

In order to carry out its role the CQC has powers of entry and inspection and power to require information, documents and records. Inspection reports are publicly available on the CQC website and anyone considering a move into residential care is encouraged to view the home's most recent report. The 2010 Regulations provide a framework against which inspections consider the quality and safety of care provided.

What do the regulations cover?

Regulation 9: care and welfare of service users
Regulation 10: assessing and monitoring the quality of service provision
Regulation 11: safeguarding service users from abuse
Regulation 12: cleanliness and infection control
Regulation 13: management of medicines
Regulation 14: meeting nutritional needs
Regulation 15: safety and suitability of premises
Regulation 16: safety and availability and suitability of equipment
Regulation 18: consent to care and treatment
Regulation 19: complaints
Regulation 20: records
Regulation 21: requirements relating to workers
Regulation 22: staffing
Regulation 23: supporting workers
Regulation 24: co-operating with other providers

It is appropriate to examine some aspects of the regulations as they relate to safeguarding and abuse in more detail.

- **Regulation 9:** proper steps must be taken to ensure each service user is protected against the risks of receiving care that is inappropriate or unsafe. This specifically includes planning care which meets individual needs; reflects research evidence and guidance as to good practice; and the avoidance of unlawful discrimination.

- **Regulation 11:** suitable arrangements must be made to ensure service users are safeguarded against the risk of abuse by taking reasonable steps to identify the possibility of it occurring and to prevent it happening; and by responding appropriately to any allegation of abuse. Abuse is defined as: sexual; physical or psychological ill-treatment; theft, misuse or misappropriation of money or property; neglect and acts of omission which cause harm or place the person at risk of harm. The practice of restraint is specifically mentioned with a requirement that, if used, there must be suitable arrangements to protect against it being unlawful or otherwise excessive.
- **Regulation 13:** appropriate arrangements must be made for obtaining, recording, handling, using, safe-keeping, safe administration and disposal of medicines.
- **Regulation 17:** suitable arrangements must be made to ensure service users' dignity, privacy and independence, and their participation in decisions relating to their care and treatment. In making such arrangements the regulation echoes elements of the MCA 2005 principles, as the service user must be provided with appropriate information and support; encouraged to understand choices, including the balance of risks and benefits involved in a particular course of care or treatment, and to express choices. This regulation also reflects social work values with reference to the need to treat service users with consideration and respect; promote autonomy, independence and community involvement and ensure care and treatment is provided with due regard for service users' age, sex, religious persuasion, sexual orientation, racial origin, cultural and linguistic background and any disability.
- **Regulation 19:** there must an effective complaints system in place for identifying, receiving, handling and responding appropriately to complaints and comments made by service users or people acting on their behalf (see further, Chapter 6).

The Care Quality Commission (Registration) Regulations 2009 provide additional requirements that the registered person must comply with.

In particular, the registered person must notify the CQC without delay of the death of a service user and if any of the following incidents occur: any injury to a service user; any deprivation of liberty request; any abuse or allegation of abuse; any incident which is reported to or investigated by the police; anything which is likely to prevent the service provider's ability to carry on the regulated activity safely, including shortage of staff, interruption of utility supplies, physical damage to the property and failure of alarms.

Enforcement action

The CQC has a range of enforcement powers against the registered person and its *Enforcement Policy* (2013a) is available on the CQC website. The range of regulatory action often starts with a request for compliance. If the problem remains, the CQC must issue a warning notice before further enforcement action can be taken. Enforcement may then follow a criminal route.

The CQC can issue a penalty notice requiring payment of a fixed penalty for an offence; a simple caution; or it may commence a prosecution. Failure to comply with the regulations is an offence and it is an offence to run a home if not registered.

Civil route

The CQC may impose, vary or remove conditions of registration. Conditions may cover the type of care provided and the profile of residents. The CQC may suspend registration and as the ultimate sanction it may cancel registration, making it illegal for the person to continue to run the home. There are also urgent procedures. Where it appears there will be serious risk to a person's life, health or well-being a magistrate may grant an order of urgent cancellation which takes immediate effect. Section 17 Health and Social Care Act 2008 sets out the grounds for cancellation of registration of a person ('R'), including: R has been convicted of or admitted a relevant offence; any other person has been convicted of a relevant offence in relation to the regulated activity; the regulated activity has not been carried out in accordance with relevant requirements, i.e. conditions or regulations. There is a right to make representations and to appeal against any of the civil compliance measures.

Tribunal decisions

If a prospective manager is refused initial registration, or registration is cancelled (including urgent cancellation), or they wish to question any conditions imposed, then an application may be made to the First-Tier

Tribunal (Health, Education and Social Care) formerly known as the Care Standards Tribunal. The tribunal comprises a chairperson from a legal background and two other members with relevant experience. Decisions of the tribunal set out the facts of each case clearly and detail the evidence provided, often commenting on credibility of witnesses and the role of the regulatory body. They are a clear source of evidence of instances of institutional abuse, as the following recent examples illustrate.

In *MNS Care plc v CQC* [2013], warning notices were issued by CQC to the home. Concerns related to failure to manage care of individuals with pressure sores; failure to assess service users correctly to minimize the risk of inadequate nutrition and hydration; staff shortages and inadequate systems relating to investigation and reporting of injuries within the adults at risk safeguarding policy. The homeowner appealed against the imposition of a condition on registration to the effect that the 'registered provider must not admit any service users without prior written agreement of the Commission'. The tribunal confirmed that the condition was appropriate and should remain in force for six months during which time the owner should work towards compliance with standards.

MM v CQC [2012] concerned an appeal against the refusal of registration of a proposed manager of a care home for the elderly. The CQC held a fit person interview and was concerned at a pattern of offending behaviour including being drunk in charge of a seven-year-old child. The tribunal considered each of the offences and granted the appeal finding that the appellant had a good work record, showed remorse and was of sufficiently good character to be registered as manager of the home.

In *Oluko v CQC* [2012] a carer in a residential home had concerns about the way residents were treated. She wore a concealed video camera and recorded instances of abuse which led to suspension of eight staff and two convictions under s. 44 MCA 2005 (ill-treatment and wilful neglect). Oluku appealed against cancellation of her registration as manager of the home. The CQC was of the opinion that she did not fulfil reg. 6(2)(b) 2010 Regulations which requires managers to be 'physically and mentally fit to carry on the regulated activity and [have] the necessary skills and experience to do so'. In addition the CQC alleged that she failed to ensure the welfare of service users as she permitted shouting at service users and allowed some to be locked in their rooms; failed to safeguard service users from abuse, failed to refer to doctors and failed to report an incident of sexual abuse; medicines were given at the wrong times for the convenience of staff rather than good health of residents;

there were insufficient meaningful activities for dementia sufferers who were restrained by removal of seat cushions and allowed to wander and shout irrespective of safety or need; and residents were all put to bed at 7.30pm as the only way she could run the home on limited staff.

The tribunal observed that:

> Residents had choices removed from them, simple matters such as whether they could take an afternoon nap, whether they wished to come down for breakfast, as we saw on video whether they removed their teeth for washing or it was done in place, whether they could stand up when they wished, by removing cushions from chairs, whether they should sit on the toilet at a particular time.
>
> Oluko v CQC [2012] [27]

The appeal was dismissed. The tribunal recognized some positives in the appellant and noted that she felt unsupported by her staff and management committee but nevertheless stated:

> We find that the appellant, despite her undoubted commitment and organizational abilities, and enthusiasm and sense of responsibility does not have the necessary skills required under regulation 6(2) because of a weakness in being able to engender in her staff a culture of being able to deal with all of the needs of the residents in a proportionate manner, and an inability to ensure that they do so.
>
> Oluko v CQC [2012] [30]

This tribunal also hears appeals against decisions of the HCPC about social work conduct.

Concerns about the CQC

In recent years the CQC has adopted a 'lighter touch' approach to inspections and its available workforce has been reduced. In this context concerns have been expressed with Sutherland and Leatherman (2006) suggesting that inspectors adopted a tick-box compliance methodology. Mandelstam (2013) identified numerous examples of approved providers where serious failings in care provided transpired. In *Clark (t/a Rosecroft Rest Home) v CQC* [2012], the tribunal noted 'long standing systematic failures in the management of the Home' and expressed concern regarding the CQC that issues had been raised about the home for some time but no action had been taken. Further, and perhaps most shocking, Winterbourne View Hospital was recorded to be complying with standards at the time the undercover investigation revealed serious concerns. In response, the CQC (2013d) has published plans to change the way it monitors, inspects and regulates adult social care services.

PRACTICE FOCUS

Ann is becoming increasingly worried about John's care in a residential home and has started to keep a diary when she visits. She has listed the following concerns:

- John often wears clothes that do not belong to him;
- she is asked to leave at meal times;
- when she arrived at 7pm one evening all the residents were in bed;
- a woman in the room opposite uses a commode in full view of anyone passing along the corridor;
- the notes of John's medication are incomplete;
- his watch has gone missing;
- he seems very nervous in the company of one of the care staff, a young man called Jim;
- his lips are chapped and he is often thirsty;
- his bed sheets are dirty; and
- there are no activities for residents other than television in the main lounge.

The final straw comes when she notices he has a large bruise on his shoulder. The home manager says that John slipped when Jim was helping him into bed. Ann asks exactly when this happened and was told that they only keep records of serious incidents.

- How should Ann's concerns be addressed?

Whistleblowing

Some safeguarding cases are brought to the attention of the local authority and other bodies via the actions of a 'whistleblower', an obvious recent example being the former senior nurse at Winterbourne View Hospital, Terry Bryan. The idea of whistleblowing is arguably supported by Article 10 ECHR:

Article 10

1. Everyone has the right to freedom of expression. This right shall include freedom to hold opinions and to receive and impart information and ideas without interference by public authority and regardless of frontiers.

2. The exercise of these freedoms, since it carries with it duties and responsibilities, may be subjected to such formalities, restrictions or penalties as are prescribed by law and are necessary in a democratic society, in the interests of national security, territorial integrity or public safety, for the prevention of disorder or crime, for the protection of health or morals, for the protection of the reputation or rights of others, for preventing the disclosure of information received in confidence, or for maintaining the authority and impartiality of the judiciary.

Human Rights Act 1998

As this is a qualified Article, the determination of whether a breach has occurred will include consideration of the individual right and general public interest and the application of proportionality. For example, the extent to which disclosure of confidential information will be protected will depend partly on the reason for disclosure and whether it fulfils a pressing social need. An example is provided in the case of *Heinisch v Germany* [2011]. The court found that Article 10 ECHR was breached where a geriatric nurse had been dismissed following her complaint about the provision of institutional care by her employer.

No Secrets refers to whistleblowing at para 6.2 which reads:

> it is the responsibility of all staff to act on any suspicion or evidence of abuse or neglect (see the PIDA 1998) and to pass on their concerns to a responsible person/agency. (DH, 2000b:6.2)

Full legal recognition is found in the Public Interest Disclosure Act 1998, which amends the Employment Rights Act 1996 to provide some employment protection to those who whistleblow responsibly.

A person who makes a 'qualifying disclosure' believing it to be true should not be dismissed or disciplined and will be entitled to complain to the Employment Tribunal if they suffer any detriment by their employer (s. 103 Employment Rights Act 1996). Since the introduction of the Enterprise and Regulatory Reform Act 2013, a whistleblower will be required to show that they reasonably believe the disclosure is in the public interest (replacing the previous requirement that disclosures were made 'in good faith').

A qualifying disclosure is one which relates to one or more of the following areas:

- a criminal offence;
- failure to comply with a legal obligation;
- a miscarriage of justice;
- danger to the health and safety of any individual;
- damage to the environment; or
- deliberate concealment of information that would show any of the previous categories (s. 43b Employment Rights Act 1996)

Protection does not extend to a whistleblower's misconduct – for example, in the form of computer hacking to prove the concern in *Bolton School v Evans* [2006].

Disclosures made internally (e.g. to senior management) or to the regulatory body (e.g. the CQC) will be protected. In circumstances where internal disclosure would not be appropriate, external disclosure may be protected. Internal disclosure may not be appropriate where the issue is particularly serious, where a previous disclosure has been effective or where internal disclosure may enable a cover-up of the wrongdoing.

Any attempt in an employment agreement to prevent workers making protected disclosures (sometimes referred to as gagging clauses) will be void under s. 43J. As well as liability on the part of the employer, protection has been extended so that if an individual is bullied or harassed by fellow employees those individuals may have personal liability for victimization of a whistleblower (Enterprise and Regulatory Reform Act 2013). This appears to be a response to the case of *Fecitt and Others v Manchester NHS* [2011]. Here, nurses who had disclosed a colleague's false claims of qualification were victimized by other co-workers. The Court of Appeal ruled that, unlike the scheme provided by the Equality Act 2010 applicable to victimization of an individual claiming discrimination, there was no liability on individual workers for victimization and hence no vicarious liability by the employer for their acts.

Despite the legal protection outlined for whistleblowers there may be many reasons why an individual would be reluctant to make a disclosure, including: fear of reprisals; concern about future employment prospects; concern that others may be implicated and possibly harmed, e.g. residents in a nursing home; and concern that disclosures will not be believed or acted upon. Against these concerns there are the potential benefits of immediate protection of individuals in some situations and changes that may result from the challenge to bad practice. Most recently, Francis (2013) endorsed the need for effective whistleblowing and complaints procedures.

Support and advice for individuals who blow the whistle is available from PCAW, an independent body established in 1993 with an advice line. Its recent report (PCAW and University of Greenwich, 2013) profiles experiences of 1000 whistleblowers. Key findings include:

- individuals are more likely to raise concerns internally than externally;
- 83 per cent of workers blew the whistle at least twice;
- 74 per cent said nothing was done about the wrongdoing;
- 60 per cent received no response at all from management;
- 15 per cent were dismissed;
- newer employees (in post less than two years) were more likely to whistleblow;
- whistleblowing concerns are raised most often in health, care services, education, charities, local government and financial services.

On-the-spot question	Given the existence and role of the regulatory body, CQC, why do some cases of serious abuse remain undetected until exposed by a whistleblower?

Further reading

These resources consider professionalism of staff and abuse in residential settings. The Winterbourne serious case review and CQC response are highly recommended reading.

Clapton, K (2013) 'Developing professional boundaries guidance for social workers' 15(1) *Journal of Adult Protection* 37

Flynn, M and V Citarella (2012) *Winterbourne View Hospital: A Serious Case Review*

Hussein, S et al. (2009) 'Accusations of misconduct amongst staff working with vulnerable adults in England' 31(1) *Journal of Social Welfare and Family Law* 17

McLaughlin, K (2010) 'The social worker versus the General Social Care Council: an analysis of Care Standards Tribunal hearings and decisions' 40 *British Journal of Social Work* 311

Marsland, D, P Oakes and C White (2007) 'Abuse in care? The identification of early indicators of the abuse of people with learning disabilities in residential settings' 9(4) *Journal of Adult Protection* 6

Mustafa, N (2008) 'How the United Kingdom's Criminal Records Bureau can reduce the prevalence of elder abuse by improving recruitment decision-making' 10(4) *Journal of Adult Protection* 37

Rosenbach, A (2011) *Internal Management Review of the Regulation of Winterbourne View*

6

OTHER LEGAL PROVISION

AT A GLANCE THIS CHAPTER COVERS:

- the role of the civil law of tort and contract
- gifts and undue influence
- domestic violence injunctions
- forced marriage
- complaints
- section 47 National Assistance Act 1948
- powers of entry
- Trading standards and environmental health issues
- housing
- mental health law
- Equality Act 2010

Given the nature of the range and diversity of law which may be relevant to safeguarding adults it is perhaps not surprising to find a chapter which sweeps up provisions that fall beyond the key areas already discussed of prevention, criminal law, capacity and regulation. The relevance of some of the issues discussed in this chapter may not be immediately apparent, yet they offer some important options.

In addition to the major areas of law covered in earlier chapters, this chapter will consider aspects of civil law, including tort, contract, domestic violence injunctions, law relating to forced marriage, complaints and the role of the Local Government Ombudsman (LGO), trading standards, housing, powers of entry, removal under the Mental Health Act 1983 and the National Assistance Act 1948 and duties under the Equality Act 2010.

Civil law: tort

The law of tort, a collective term for civil wrongs, comprises the following torts that may have an application in safeguarding cases: negligence, assault and battery (trespass to the person) and false imprisonment. Detailed examination of the law of tort is beyond the scope of this text – for further reference there are numerous legal textbooks focusing on this area of law (e.g. Horsey and Rackley, 2013).

At the outset it is important to note that the usual remedy in tort is damages, i.e. a financial compensation payment. On occasion, injunctions may be used to prevent further acts. In *Patel v Patel* [1988], a son-in-law abused and damaged the property of his father-in-law and harassed him by telephone calls and visits to the property. A non-molestation injunction with a 50-yard exclusion zone was ordered. Such a case would be more likely to be dealt with now under the Family Law Act 1996 given the extended category of associated persons. It is possible for the same behaviour to give rise to both civil and criminal behaviour as in the Practice Focus below (see page 124).

Negligence

These are the essential elements to an action in negligence:

- duty: a duty of care exists to prevent certain damage occurring;
- breach: breach of the duty, conduct falls below a reasonable standard of care;

> ### PRACTICE FOCUS
>
> Anne visits her mother in a care home, catches her foot on some loose carpet and falls, banging her head and suffering brain damage as a result, meaning she will never work again in her profession as a barrister. The care home is prosecuted by the CQC for breach of regulations (criminal action).
>
> Anne receives damages for the care home's negligence (civil). Her mother is also able to claim damages for psychological harm having witnessed the incident.

- causation: the breach is directly causative of the damage;
- damage: the claimant actually suffered damage.

Actions are frequently brought against the NHS (and others) for medical or clinical negligence. Cases may be settled out of court as, for example, occurred in respect of the deaths of individuals following neglect at the Mid Staffordshire NHS Foundation Trust (Francis, 2013). Negligent acts are also referred to in other legislation. For example, the protection offered under s. 5 MCA 2005, acts in connection with care or treatment (see Chapter 4), is lost if the act is carried out negligently. In extreme situations the concept of neglect also features in the criminal law. The new offence, introduced by the MCA 2005, refers to ill-treatment and wilful neglect of a person who lacks capacity, discussed in more detail in Chapter 3.

A basic consideration in law prior to any civil action concerns the likely outcome or, in other words, whether it is worth suing. If negligence was at the hands of a care assistant of limited income and means, then practically it is unlikely that a large award of damages will be obtained. The answer may lie in vicarious liability which may arise in respect of the negligent acts of another person. Generally speaking an employer will be vicariously liable for the negligent acts of employees. Thus it might be more worthwhile to sue the employer of the care assistant.

Until relatively recently some public bodies have enjoyed immunity from negligence claims. In respect of local authorities (as major employers of social workers) this is no longer true. It is possible that a service user could sue the local authority for the negligent acts of an employee, including social workers.

> **KEY CASE ANALYSIS**

Z v UK (2001)

Initially the House of Lords ruled that a local authority was immune from negligence claims (*X (Minors) v Bedfordshire County Council* [1995]). The case proceeded to the European Court of Human Rights as *Z v UK*. The court found the UK in breach of Article 3 ECHR, the right not to be subjected to inhuman or degrading treatment, for its failure to protect the children in this case from long-term abuse and neglect. As the House of Lords had struck out the negligence claims, the European Court also found the UK in breach of Article 13 ECHR as the children were denied effective redress for the breach of Article 3 ECHR. The court awarded damages and costs.

Subsequently, in *E v UK (Application 33218/96)* [2003], four children had been physically and sexually abused by their mother's partner over several years. They were awarded compensation for negligence from the local authority which had failed to protect the children.

These cases concern child abuse where there are clear statutory duties imposed on local authorities to take protective measures. It is highly arguable that the same principles would apply if a local authority were aware of abuse to a vulnerable adult and failed to act. The positive obligation to prevent individuals suffering degrading and inhuman treatment under Article 3 ECHR reinforces this point.

If negligence applies to the actions of local authorities, an obvious question to ask is: what is the standard that applies to the duty of care? Expectations of professional conduct will be relevant as set out, for example, in the Professional Capabilities Framework (The College of Social Work, 2012) and the HCPC *Standards of Proficiency* (2012), e.g. Standard 2 to be able to practise within the legal and ethical boundaries of their profession. Case law has provided some further clarification. In *ABB v Milton Keynes Council* [2011], the court ruled:

> A social worker's duty in common with other professionals is to exercise reasonable skill and care ... [she] will not be negligent if she acts in accordance with practice accepted as proper, by a responsible body of social work opinion, even though another social worker might adopt a different practice.

Trespass to the person

The tort of trespass to the person encompasses assault and battery. Whilst these terms are more often associated with criminal law, civil liability may also follow. As an example, to conduct surgery without consent of the patient (other than in emergency circumstances) would constitute assault and battery. An assault occurs where the individual has reasonable cause to fear direct harm, e.g. shaking a fist at someone. In battery there is actual direct and intentional application of force, though it does not have to involve a great degree of force, e.g. cutting a person's hair without permission. The inherent jurisdiction and declaratory powers exercisable under the MCA 2005 can provide authority for surgery and other procedures, where the patient is not able to consent and provide a defence against civil liability.

False imprisonment

False imprisonment is the infliction of physical restraint which is not authorized by law. As with assault and battery it may also result in a criminal prosecution.

A key question with any restraint will be whether it is authorized by law. Again it is relevant to consider s. 5 MCA 2005, acts in connection with care or treatment. Restraint will not be justified under this section unless D believes it is necessary to prevent harm to P and it is a proportionate response to the likelihood and seriousness of P suffering harm. Thus restraining a person from walking into the path of a moving vehicle is likely to be justified, restraining a person because it is more convenient and quicker for staff to feed the person is unlikely to be justified. If the restraint becomes a deprivation of liberty this would be covered by s. 4A MCA 2005, as discussed in Chapter 4.

Employment protection

The local authority (or other social worker employer) owes a duty of care to its employees. If negligent in employment practices there may be circumstances where the social worker as employee could succeed in an action of negligence against their employer and obtain compensation. Two cases in adult services are illustrative. In *Colclough v Staffordshire County Council* [1994], a social worker was injured trying to lift a heavy service user who had fallen out of bed. Her employer was found negligent as it had not delivered any training or information about safe manual handling. A residential social worker was injured in *Harvey v Northumberland County Council* [2003] and here the employer was negligent having failed to provide training in restraint techniques.

Employers also have responsibilities under the Health and Safety at Work Act 1974 regarding safety, health and welfare of employees, notably s. 2 includes the requirement to provide such information, instruction, training and supervision as is necessary to ensure the health and safety at work of employees. Poor employment practices, such as failure to provide appropriate training and support for staff may also be the subject of whistleblowing disclosures.

Contract and undue influence

If an individual enters into a contract under duress or undue influence he or she will not be bound by its terms. This principle is particularly relevant in relation to financial and property abuse. The remedy will usually be to set the contract aside, returning the parties to their pre-contract state, and may also include damages. A will entered into under undue influence may also be invalid. Undue influence may be actual or presumed and can include a range of conduct such as coercion, emotional blackmail, fraudulent misrepresentation, victimization, and excessive pressure and bullying. If the person who benefits from the transaction is unable to rebut the presumption of undue influence, then the transaction can be set aside.

In *Hammond v Osborn* [2002] a presumption of undue influence arose as a consequence of the relationship of trust between an elderly bachelor and his carer. He transferred around £300,000, representing over 90 per cent of his assets, to his carer of fairly recent acquaintance. The court found that it was for the carer to rebut the presumption of undue influence. It was significant that the man had not obtained any independent advice, evidence of which could have demonstrated that he made the transfer of his own free will. Further, in *Hart v Burbidge* [2013] the court found presumed undue influence in a relationship of mother and daughter. The mother transferred money to her daughter and son-in-law which enabled them to buy a property. She lived in the house with them before she died but it was only registered in the names of the daughter and her husband. As a consequence her son's share of the inheritance was much reduced.

Contract law is also relevant to local authority practice in commissioning services from the independent and private sector. Where services are contracted out, the local authority sets terms of the contract, with e.g. a domiciliary care provider, and retains a responsibility to monitor the contract and ensure that the local authority budget is spent effectively. The serious case review following the death of Mrs Gloria Foster (Surrey Safeguarding Adults Board, 2013) includes discussion of the local authority contracting role. Carefirst 24 was contracted to provide domiciliary care in the local authority area. The agency was closed following an immigration raid and Mrs Foster who had been receiving four care visits daily was found in a state of dehydration after nine days without any visits. The local authority had not made any contact with Mrs Foster to provide advice, information or alternative care and support.

Discussion of personalization in Chapter 1 includes reference to the contract of employment between an individual and their personal assistant. The Advisory, Conciliation and Arbitration Service offers useful advice on employing personal care workers on its website (www.acas.org.uk).

Domestic violence

There is an obvious relationship between domestic violence and safeguarding, although a range of factors may effect whether abuse between two adults is conceptualized as a domestic violence or a safeguarding concern. Structures for dealing with domestic violence, and particularly the role of the police, are more clearly established in relation to domestic violence. A representative of the local MARAC (Multi-Agency Risk Assessment Conferences for victims of domestic violence at high risk of serious assault or homicide) may be a useful member of the SAB.

The Home Office issued a revised definition of domestic violence in 2012 as:

> any incident or pattern of incidents of controlling, coercive, threatening behaviour, violence or abuse between those aged 16 or over who are, or have been, intimate partners or family members regardless of gender or sexuality. The abuse can encompass, but is not limited to: psychological, physical, sexual, financial, emotional. (Home Office, 2012:19)

The key legislation applying to domestic violence is the Family Law Act 1996 as amended by the Domestic Violence, Crime and Victims Act 2004. The Family Law Act 1996 significantly expanded the availability of domestic violence injunctions (non-molestation orders and occupation orders) beyond situations where abuse took place between spouses or cohabitees. Availability of the provisions of the Act depends on whether the abuse is caused by an associated person of the victim. Section 62 provides the definition of an associated person. Categories include the people set out below:

- spouses or former spouses;
- civil partners or former civil partners;
- cohabitees or former cohabitees including same-sex couples;
- persons in intimate relationship of significant duration but not living together;
- persons who have agreed to marry;
- parents of or persons who have parental responsibility for a child;
- persons living in the same household (not as employees, tenants lodgers or boarders);
- relatives – the father, mother, stepfather, stepmother, son, daughter, stepson, stepdaughter, grandmother, grandfather, grandson or granddaughter, brother, sister, uncle, aunt, niece, nephew or first cousin (whether of the full blood or of the half-blood by marriage or civil partnership);
- relatives of the person's spouse or former spouse, civil partner or former civil partner, cohabitee or former cohabitee.

In theory, just about every close family relationship in which violence may occur is now included. Informal carers such as friends or neighbours would not be included unless there was a former relationship or they lived in the household. The individual victim of domestic violence must apply directly to court for injunctive relief and may require significant support to do so. It is not currently possible for a body, such as a local authority, to apply on the victim's behalf. There is provision for this within the Family Law Act 1996 but it has not been implemented. The Legal Aid, Sentencing and Punishment of Offenders Act 2012 has restricted availability of legal aid, however, it does continue to be available for domestic violence applications. The appropriateness of orders has been questioned, however, they may provide some short-term relief.

Domestic violence support services have tended to focus on younger women, particularly where children are affected. It is clear, however, that older women do also experience violence whether this is conceptualized as domestic abuse or elder abuse and whether it has been a long-term feature within a relationship or coincided with the onset of older age.

> ◢ **PRACTICE FOCUS**
>
> Maureen stopped visiting John and Ann to spend more time with her husband on his retirement. He died suddenly and she lived alone for a while, becoming increasingly isolated. A few months ago her nephew Ian moved in to help with bills. She had not had much contact with him since he was a child but he came to the funeral and was very helpful following her husband's death. Maureen rarely leaves the house since her bereavement and is rather anxious. She gets on well with Ian most of the time but his promises to pay some keep have not materialized and she is concerned that he drinks heavily. He arrived home late last night, dragged Maureen out of bed and struck her when she refused to make him a meal. Maureen now feels quite scared of Ian and would like him to move out but worries about how she would cope alone.
>
> • What law might assist Maureen?

Forced marriage

The question of whether an individual can consent to marriage has been discussed earlier in relation to mental capacity and the emergence of the Munby vulnerable adult. It is arguable that forced marriage is a distinct form of adult abuse to which safeguarding procedures should apply.

The Forced Marriage (Civil Protection) Act 2007 provides civil remedies and the law has been extended recently to make forced marriage a criminal offence. The exact prevalence of forced marriage is difficult to ascertain and it remains a largely hidden problem (Kazimirski et al., 2008). Research by the National Centre for Social Research (Department for Children, Schools and Families (DCSF), 2009) suggests a national prevalence of reported cases of forced marriage estimated to be between 5000 and 8000 cases, predominantly affecting women and girls from Asian communities. The Act introduces a new Part 4A into the Family Law Act 1996.

Forced marriage is defined in the Family Law Act 1996 as:

s. 63A(4)

> a person (A) is forced into a marriage if another person (B) forces A to enter into a marriage (whether or not with B or another person) without A's free and full consent.

Family Law Act 1996

The conduct forcing A to enter into the marriage may be directed against A or another person.

The court may make a forced marriage protection order with discretion as to appropriate measures (prohibitions, restrictions or requirements) to include protecting a person from being forced into marriage or protecting a person who has already been forced into a marriage. Examples from the guidance (MoJ, 2009) include requirements to handover passports, stop intimidation and violence, reveal the whereabouts of a person and prevent someone being taken abroad. In deciding whether to exercise its powers, the court must have regard to the need to secure the health, safety and well-being of the person to be protected. When violence is threatened or used, a power of arrest may be attached. The court may make without notice orders in an emergency and can vary, discharge or extend existing orders.

Proceedings may be brought by the victim, another person with leave and a relevant third party, which, significantly, since 2009 has included local authorities (Family Law Act 1996 (Forced Marriage) (Relevant Third Party) Order 2009). The new law is supported by the Forced Marriage Unit (FMU), a joint initiative between the Foreign and Commonwealth Office and the Home Office, providing support to individuals and to professionals working with cases of forced marriage. The Anti-social Behaviour, Crime and Policing Act 2014 makes forced marriage a crime and makes breach of a forced marriage protection order a criminal offence. Until implemented breaches are dealt with as a civil contempt of court.

Complaints

Availability of complaints procedures provides a measure of accountability and opportunity to promote good practice. The scheme for complaints relating to adult services is contained in the Local Authority Social Services and National Health Services (England) Complaints Regulations 2009. Complaints about matters arising in the previous 12 months may be made verbally or in writing and the regulations set out timescales in which the authority must respond. There are three stages: informal, formal and review stage. If it is not possible for the complaint to be resolved informally then a panel with an independent element will be involved. The usual outcomes of a complaint are recommendations and accompanying reasons to the local authority. The local authority will keep a record of complaints received and publishes an annual report of complaints and outcomes.

Beyond the complaints procedure it is possible to take the complaint to the LGO. As a last resort the complaint may lead to a judicial review in which the court considers the decision-making of the local authority.

Local Government Ombudsman

The LGO investigates complaints against local authorities to assess whether there has been maladministration which causes an injustice to the complainant. Cases are reported on the LGO website under different categories of local authority areas of work, e.g. education, planning, social services. The LGO may make recommendations to the local authority, including suggested compensation awards. The role of the LGO was extended recently to include power to investigate complaints in relation to providers of self-funded care (by the individual's own means, direct payment or individual budget). A number of cases involve delays in assessment (*Report of an investigation into Complaint No 11 009 273 about Birmingham City Council*, 2012) and provision of services (*Report of an Investigation into Complaint No 12 007 311 against Shropshire Council*, 2013).

> ### KEY CASE ANALYSIS
>
> *Report of an Investigation into Complaint No 11 009 473 against Kent County Council*, 2012
>
> This case concerned a safeguarding investigation.
>
> Mrs B complained that the council failed to properly investigate how her father was injured during an altercation with another resident in his care home, gave her information that was wrong and failed to keep her father safe and that the care home failed to give her information about incidents involving her father. Over the course of a year a safeguarding investigation, a complaints investigation, an internal council investigation and a second internal investigation prompted by the complaint to the LGO took place. The LGO found that Mrs B had suffered distress waiting for a credible investigation and a feeling of injustice that her father's death could have been avoided. The LGO recommended the council pay £5000 compensation, a further £1000 in recognition of her time and trouble in identifying systemic weaknesses in parts of Kent's adult social care and £1500 to pay for a memorial for her father. The report details failings in the process with reference to the local authority's policy which states that abuse by one vulnerable adult of another within a service setting should be dealt with as an adult protection issue.

Section 47 National Assistance Act 1948

A local authority may apply to court for an order authorizing the removal of an individual to suitable premises. The power applies in respect of a person who is:

- suffering from grave chronic disease, or being aged, infirm or physically incapacitated, is living in insanitary conditions; and
- unable to devote to themselves, and is not receiving from other persons, proper care and attention.

There is no requirement that the person is mentally ill or mentally disordered. On the face of it the provision appears to fit cases of self-neglect through inclusion of the phrase 'unable to devote to themselves', however, it seems that the power is rarely used in, and only in, circumstances of last resort. It is likely that its use could be challenged under Articles 5, 6 and 8 ECHR. The Law Commission recommended its abolition and the Care Act 2014 provides for its repeal.

Power of entry

Some respondents to the Law Commission (2011b) (and the *No Secrets* review, DH, 2008a; 2009) accepted the need to abolish s. 47 National Assistance Act but suggested that local authorities did need some powers to gain access to an individual for the purpose of carrying out safeguarding enquiries. A separate consultation was conducted on whether a new power of entry should be developed (DH, 2012)

Although the proposal was apparently supported by a majority of respondents, the government response to this consultation concluded that a safeguarding power of entry was unnecessary (DH, 2013). The table in Chapter 8 shows that this leaves England without such a power in contrast to the established position in Scotland and reforms in Wales.

The Police and Criminal Evidence Act 1984 provides a power of entry to the police to enter and search premises without a warrant in order to save life or limb or prevent serious damage to property (s. 17(1)(e)). This section would only apply in cases where there were really serious concerns for the safety of an individual.

Environmental health

Section 47 National Assistance Act 1948 includes a reference to insanitary conditions. There may be cases where, alongside concerns for an individual's well-being and possible neglect, they are also at risk because of their living conditions. Cases of hoarding, where individuals accumulate possessions and rubbish, sometimes associated with obsessive compulsive disorder, have attracted media attention and some local authorities have hoarder policies.

The Public Health Act 1936 provides local authorities with powers in respect of premises, which are filthy, unwholesome or verminous, verminous articles and verminous people or clothing. The council in exercising its powers may obtain an order from the magistrates to enter premises and can remove the person during fumigation (ss 83–85).

Local authorities also have powers of entry in cases of statutory nuisance under the Environmental Protection Act 1990. Statutory nuisance is defined in s. 79 and includes:

- premises in a state prejudicial to health or nuisance;
- smoke, fumes or gases emitted from premises so as to be prejudicial to health or a nuisance;
- any accumulation or deposit prejudicial to health or a nuisance;
- any animal kept in such a place or manner as to be prejudicial to health or a nuisance;
- noise emitted from premises so as to be prejudicial to health or a nuisance.

The local authority can enter premises to ascertain whether a nuisance exists, having given 24 hours' notice for a residential property. If a statutory nuisance is found, the authority serves an abatement notice and, if the nuisance is not abated, the local authority may take action itself.

Under both the Public Health Act 1936 and the Environmental Protection Act 1990 the local authority may obtain an order from the magistrates providing a power of entry to premises, using force where necessary.

Trading standards

Trading standards has a role in relation to complaints about bogus callers or rogue traders and is able to initiate criminal prosecutions. Trading standards may be involved in community safety partnerships and have a preventive role alongside its powers to prosecute.

R v Baker [2011] provides an example of a large-scale fraud. The judgment begins with a summary of the facts which refer to:

> … a team of rogue builders who defrauded householders in the south east of England by undertaking repair work to houses, in particular roofs and chimneys, which was unnecessary, dishonestly charging for work which was not carried out, carrying out incompetent and sub-standard work, and claiming to have carried out work which was not in fact done. Over a period from January 2003 until September 2007 about 43 householders were defrauded and about £800,000 was obtained. Smith was involved throughout the conspiracy. The offences followed a very similar pattern. The victims were nearly all either elderly or otherwise vulnerable householders. They would be cold-called and told that work was required, usually to their roof or chimney, and that it required immediate attention. A price would be quoted for the work, but as soon as the work commenced, further, more substantial, problems were found, and they were said to require immediate attention. The work carried out would be cosmetic and unnecessary, and the amount charged for the work would be grossly excessive. Any work which was carried out would be to a very poor standard and frequently required rectification by competent contractors, and work which was supposed to have been carried out never was.
>
> R v Baker *[2011] [3]*

One of the builders was convicted of obtaining and attempting to obtain property by deception and sentenced to seven years' imprisonment.

Following a report by the Law Commission (2012), the government stated its intention to amend the law with the introduction of the Consumer Protection from Unfair Trading (Amendment) Regulations 2013, which make it easier for victims of rogue traders to get their money back. The regulations will give consumers: 90 days to cancel a contract and receive a full refund if they have been misled or bullied into agreeing to it; new rights to recover money paid but not owed; and a right to claim compensation for alarm or distress.

Housing

Housing is important in two key respects in relation to safeguarding. First, housing law is important to the many vulnerable adults living in a range of housing. Second, housing providers need to have a firm place in multi-agency approaches to safeguarding, though currently Parry suggests that housing organizations vary in the extent to which they have engaged in the safeguarding adults agenda (2013:17). The case of *R (Weaver) v L & Q Housing Trust* [2009] confirms that most registered providers of social housing are considered to be exercising a public function under the terms of the Human Rights Act 1998 and must thus act compatibly with the ECHR.

It is important to recognize that, while some vulnerable adults live in sheltered or supported housing, where staff should have an awareness of safeguarding, many other vulnerable adults live in general needs housing (Parry, 2013). Such was the case for Steven Hoskin whose serious case review identified the housing authority as one of the agencies that missed the opportunity to intervene and at least refer to safeguarding (Flynn, 2007).

Relevant law includes the Family Law Act 1996, the Anti-Social Behaviour Act 2003, the Crime and Disorder Act 1998 and the Housing Act 1996, key elements of which are summarized below. This is a complex area of law where further specialist advice will often be required.

- Under the Family Law Act 1996, an occupation order can be made determining who can live in a property. As a type of injunction it can allow a person to stay in the home or return to it and prevent a person from entering the home or a stipulated area in the neighbourhood. The applicant must be an associated person as discussed above, in a range of circumstances including cases where there is no legal right to occupy the property. They are intended to be short-term orders (up to six months) put in place whilst other arrangements are made. A power of arrest may be attached to the order. Domestic violence applications are one of the few areas of civil law where legal aid is still available since the reforms of the Legal Aid, Sentencing and Punishment of Offenders Act 2012.
- The Housing Act 1996 (amended by the Homelessness Act 2002) provides the legal framework on homelessness. Anyone who is homeless or threatened with homelessness is entitled to advice and assistance

from the housing authority and in some circumstances emergency accommodation must be provided. A person will be considered homeless if it is not reasonable for them to continue to occupy a property where violence to the individual or a member of their family would result.

- Accommodation must be made available to an applicant who is homeless and has a priority need. Priority need categories include a person who is vulnerable because of a disability, physical or mental health problems and also a person who has left a property because of violence or threats of violence.
- Registered social landlords can apply for injunctions to prevent anti-social behaviour which causes nuisance or annoyance under the Anti-Social Behaviour Act 2003.
- Clauses prohibiting anti-social behaviour by tenants and guests are included in social tenancy agreements and breach may lead to eviction.
- Housing and homelessness cases will be informed by the positive duty to promote Article 8 ECHR rights.

Mental health

Support provisions under the Mental Health Act 1983 were discussed in Chapter 2. The sections of the Act relating to short and longer-term removal and detention may also be relevant in some safeguarding cases where the victim or perpetrator is suffering from a mental disorder as defined under the Act and other relevant criteria are satisfied. The emphasis is on the need for detention for the patient's safety or the protection of others, i.e. in the wider interests of society. The application of such criteria would not necessarily coincide with an assessment of best interests. Detention under the Mental Health Act 1983 is covered by one of the exceptions under Article 5 ECHR and does not violate the right to liberty provided the correct procedures are followed (*Winterwerp v The Netherlands* (1979)).

The removal and detention provisions are supported by s. 115 Mental Health Act 1983 which authorizes an Approved Mental Health Professional to enter premises in which a mentally disordered patient is living if there is reasonable cause to believe the patient is not under proper care.

The relevant provisions are set out in the table below.

Section	Criteria	Detention period
s. 2	Detention for assessment in the interests of the person's own health or safety of for the protection of others.	28 days
s. 3	Detention for treatment necessary for the person's own health or safety or for the protection of others. Appropriate treatment is available and cannot be provided unless the person is detained.	6 months
s. 4	Urgent necessity: immediate and significant risk of mental or physical harm to the person or others, danger of physical harm to property or the need for physical restraint.	72 hours
s. 5	Detention of an in-patient by a doctor or nurse.	6 hours (nurse); 72 hours (doctor)
s. 135	Police warrant to enter premises and remove to a place of safety a person who is being ill-treated, neglected or kept otherwise than under proper control, or is living alone and unable to care for him or herself.	72 hours
s. 136	Police may remove a person to a place of safety when found in a public place, where he or she is in need of care and control and removal is necessary in the person's interest or for the protection of others.	72 hours

Table 6.1: Removal and detention provisions under the Mental Health Act 1983

The detention periods detailed are maximum periods. If a person is no longer suffering from a mental disorder he or she should be discharged. Unnecessary delay in discharging a patient may violate Article 5 ECHR (*Johnson v UK* (1999) 27 EHRR 296).

The Equality Act 2010

Discriminatory abuse is specifically referred to as a category of abuse in *No Secrets* (DH, 2000b). There may be a criminal law response or measures to prevent further abuse and provide support may be relevant, but it is also appropriate to consider the legal framework for anti-discrimination which is now provided for under a single piece of legislation – the Equality Act 2010.

The new Act applies to all organizations that provide a service to the public (or section of the public) and to anyone who sells goods or provides facilities. The Act offers protection from discrimination in respect of nine areas of protected characteristics, namely: age; disability; gender reassignment; marriage and civil partnership; pregnancy and maternity; race (including ethnic or national origins, colour or nationality); religion or belief; sex; and sexual orientation. Extended forms of discrimination are recognized, including: direct discrimination; dual discrimination; discrimination by association; discrimination by perception; indirect discrimination; harassment; and victimization.

In addition to the opportunities for individuals with one or more protected characteristics to make a claim of having suffered discrimination, two specific duties are imposed on public bodies, which include social services authorities. Firstly, public bodies must have due regard to socio-economic inequalities when making decisions of a strategic nature about how to exercise their functions. Secondly, an equality duty applies, meaning that local authorities must, in the exercise of their functions, have due regard to the need to eliminate discrimination, harassment and victimization and advance equality of opportunity in respect of each of the nine areas of protected characteristics (s. 149 Equality Act 2010).

Challenges have been brought against local authorities for failure to comply with the equality duty. In *R (W) v Birmingham City Council* [2011], the authority's decision to restrict the provision of support for people with disabilities to those whose needs were assessed to be critical was unlawful. By failing to assess the practical impact on those disabled persons whose needs were substantial, the local authority had not paid due regard to the equality duty. The decision-maker should consider the impact of a proposed decision and ask whether a decision with that impact would be consistent with the need to pay due regard to the principles of disability equality.

Public bodies in England, including local authorities, are obliged to publish annual information regarding their compliance with the equality duty and also set equality objectives every four years.

On-the-spot question

Reflect upon the range of law outlined in this and the preceding chapters. Are social workers in safeguarding teams equipped with an effective and proportionate range of powers for safeguarding adults?

Further reading

ADASS and LGA (2013) *Adult Safeguarding and Domestic Abuse: A Guide to Support Practitioners and Managers* discusses the interface between the two areas of practice and provides useful illustrative case studies.

Kline, R and M Preston-Shoot (2012) *Professional Accountability in Social care and Health: Challenging Unacceptable Practice and its Management*: this book provides full coverage of a range of complaint avenues in the context of accountability.

Parry, I (2013) 'Adult safeguarding and the role of housing' 1 *Journal of Adult Protection* 15 is a detailed consideration of the actual and potential engagement of housing in safeguarding adults.

7

MESSAGES FROM SERIOUS CASE REVIEWS

AT A GLANCE THIS CHAPTER COVERS:

- the role and structure of Safeguarding Adults Boards
- safeguarding adults reviews under the Care Act 2014
- a selection of serious case reviews
- the emphasis on learning lessons from reviews

This chapter considers the role and impact of a number of serious case reviews concerning vulnerable adults. It begins with discussion of SABs, firstly, due to their involvement with serious case reviews and, secondly, recognizing that a key recommendation of many of the reviews is the need to strengthen multi-agency communication and SABs have a pivotal role to play in that issue: 'Nearly all SCR investigations highlight a breakdown in partnership working as a key factor in failing to keep people safe.' (ADASS and LGA, 2013:15) The current status of SABs and developments with the introduction of the Care Act 2014 are a preliminary consideration.

The primary aim of both serious case reviews (and safeguarding adults reviews, as introduced by the Care Act 2014) is not to apportion blame, it is to consider lessons to be learnt for the future. The chapter concludes with summaries of a selection of serious case reviews together with key findings and recommendations.

Safeguarding Adults Boards

There is currently no absolute requirement for local authorities to establish SABs (in contrast to the requirement to establish Local Safeguarding Children Boards under the Children Act 2004). Consideration of some form of board, described as a multi-agency management committee, was envisaged by *No Secrets* but not required. The guidance states:

> To achieve effective inter-agency working, agencies may consider that there are merits in establishing a multi-agency management committee (adult protection), which is a standing committee of lead officers. Such a body should have a clearly defined remit and lines of accountability, and it should identify agreed objectives and priorities for its work. Such committees should determine policy, co-ordinate activity between agencies, facilitate joint training, and monitor and review progress.
>
> *DH, 2000b:3.4*

Unsurprisingly, in the absence of a statutory requirement to establish boards, practices were inconsistent and, where boards were established, membership varied (Perkins et al., 2007). In their work on governance of adult safeguarding, Braye et al. argue that:

> Specific legislation that sets out for Safeguarding Boards roles and functions would help to standardise policy and procedures, to hold agencies more easily accountable, to clarify responsibilities and to ensure participation, in ways that guidance, differentially binding on the partners, has not so far been able to do. (2011c:185)

A consistent message emerged from the review of *No Secrets*, action of campaigning organizations and work of the Law Commission, the latter finding 'compelling reasons' in favour of adult safeguarding boards being placed on a statutory footing (Spencer-Lane, 2011). This was followed by the government statement in 2011 expressing a commitment to legislate to make SABs statutory.

A statutory requirement is now contained in the Care Act 2014, s. 43 which requires local authorities to establish an SAB:

s. 43

(1) Each local authority must establish a Safeguarding Adults Board (an 'SAB') for its area.
(2) The objective of an SAB is to help and protect adults in its area in cases of the kind described in s 42(1).
(3) The way in which an SAB must seek to achieve its objective is by co-ordinating and ensuring the effectiveness of what each of its members does.
(4) An SAB may do anything which appears to it to be necessary or desirable for the purpose of achieving its objective.
(5) Schedule 2 (which includes provision about the membership, funding and other resources, strategy and annual reporting of an SAB) has effect.

Care Act 2014

Two or more local authorities may establish an SAB for their combined area (s. 43(6)). Schedule 2 includes detail about membership and other matters. The members of an SAB are the local authority which established it, a clinical commissioning group (whole or part of which is) within the local authority's area, the chief officer of police (whole or part of which is) within the local authority's area, and others as specified in regulations. As clinical commissioning groups and police areas do not always coincide with local authority areas (and more than one local authority may combine for an SAB) there is the potential for representation by e.g. more than one chief police of police to attend. For that reason one person may represent more than one of the clinical groups or police authorities. The local authority then has a discretion to include other persons after consultation with the core group. It has been suggested that housing issues are often neglected in serious case reviews, even though vulnerable adults frequently live in supported or social housing, and that housing should be represented on SABS (Parry, 2013).

The local authority must appoint a chair of the SAB with 'required skills and experience'. Unlike the position in Scotland, since implementation of the Adult Support and Protection (Scotland) Act 2007, there is no requirement that the chair is independent of the authority (see discussion in Cornish and Preston-Shoot, 2013). In some areas the chair of the SAB may also chair the Local Safeguarding Children Board. The SAB can regulate its own procedure, subject to any guidance issued by the Secretary of State. Without such guidance, concerns about consistency across boards may continue. Significantly, this applies to the way in which SARs will be conducted and appears to ignore the consistent call of the ADASS for each local authority to have something similar to a Safeguarding Children Review protocol, dealing with when and how to commission an SAR and how they will implement and monitor the recommendations (ADSS 2006 (updated 2010); ADASS and LGA, 2013).

Each SAB must publish an annual strategic plan and an annual report. The annual report must include the findings of any SARs which have concluded in that year and any ongoing reviews.

Safeguarding adults reviews

A key duty for the SAB is to arrange for an SAR in specified circumstances. The SAR replaces the previous terminology of serious case review. There is currently no obligation to carry out and publish reviews, nor is there any obligation on agencies to cooperate.

The Care Act 2014 requirement to conduct SARs is contained in s. 44.

s. 44 Safeguarding adults reviews

(1) An SAB must arrange for there to be a review of a case involving an adult in its area with needs for care and support (whether or not the local authority has been meeting any of those needs) if—

(a) there is reasonable cause for concern about how the SAB, members of it or other persons with relevant functions worked together to safeguard the adult, and

(b) condition 1 or 2 is met.

(2) Condition 1 is met if—

(a) the adult has died, and

(b) the SAB knows or suspects that the death resulted from abuse or neglect (whether or not it knew about or suspected the abuse or neglect before the adult died).

(3) Condition 2 is met if—

(a) the adult is still alive, and

(b) the SAB knows or suspects that the adult has experienced serious abuse or neglect.

(4) An SAB may arrange for there to be a review of any other case involving an adult in its area with needs for care and support (whether or not the local authority has been meeting any of those needs).

(5) Each member of the SAB must co-operate in and contribute to the carrying out of a review under this section with a view to—

(a) identifying the lessons to be learnt from the adult's case, and

(b) applying those lessons to future cases.

Care Act 2014

Collaborative work is essential to secure a timely and coordinated response to safeguarding concerns. Regrettably, lack of or ineffective sharing of information has been a feature of both child and adult serious case reviews. A duty to cooperate imposed on bodies likely to be represented on safeguarding boards may strengthen inter-agency working within a framework of accountability to the board, and give teeth to the *No Secrets* call for 'all responsible agencies [to] work together to ensure … a consistent and effective response to any circumstances giving ground for concern' (DH, 2000b:1.2)

Section 45 sets out the circumstances when information must be supplied to an SAB:

s. 45 Supply of information

(1) If an SAB requests a person to supply information to it, or to some other person specified in the request, the person to whom the request is made must comply with the request if—

(a) conditions 1 and 2 are met, and

(b) condition 3 or 4 is met.

(2) Condition 1 is that the request is made for the purpose of enabling or assisting the SAB to exercise its functions.

(3) Condition 2 is that the request is made to a person whose functions or activities the SAB considers to be such that the person is likely to have information relevant to the exercise of a function by the SAB.

(4) Condition 3 is that the information relates to—
   (a) the person to whom the request is made,
   (b) a function or activity of that person, or
   (c) a person in respect of whom that person exercises a function or engages in an activity.

(5) Condition 4 is that the information—
   (a) is information requested by the SAB from a person to whom information was supplied in compliance with another request under this section, and
   (b) is the same as, or is derived from, information so supplied.

Care Act 2014

Schedule 2(5) Care Act 2014 requires each member of the SAB to cooperate and contribute to SARs with a view to:

   (a) identifying the lessons to be learnt from the adult's case, and
   (b) applying those lessons to future cases.

Schedule 2(5) Care Act 2014

The ADASS and the LGA suggest further that: 'the overriding reasons for holding a review must be to learn from past experience, improve future practice and multi-agency working' (2013:15)

The final section of this chapter summarizes the findings and recommendations of a selection of serious case reviews. In addition to serious case reviews it is also important to note the existence of other types of reviews to which safeguarding adults practitioners might contribute, such as: children's serious case reviews; domestic homicide reviews; multi-agency serious incident reviews; mental health homicide and suicide inquiries; and coroner's court enquiries. The inconsistency in presentation and content of reviews has already been noted. Reviews are available on local authority websites, but often only as executive summaries with full versions not always publicly available (Scourfield, 2010).

Serious case review examples

Steven Hoskin

A 39-year-old man with a learning disability was killed by two people who had 'befriended' him and effectively moved into his home and taken control of his life. Prior to his death he was forced to take paracetamol, was burnt with cigarettes, dragged around by a lead, suffered bruising to his neck and footprint marks on his hands and his ultimate cause of death was falling 30 metres from a railway viaduct. Between August 2005 and June 2006 the police had 12 contacts with him and Steven himself informed social services that he was being taken advantage of, then later cancelled his community care support. 'Each agency focused on single issues within their own sectional remits and did not make the connections deemed necessary for the protection of vulnerable adults and proposed by *No Secrets*.' (Flynn, 2007:21)

Fiona Pilkington and Francesca Hardwick

Fiona Pilkington killed herself and her 18-year-old daughter Francesca who had learning disabilities. They had endured prolonged harassment from youths on their housing estate. The case was treated as an instance of anti-social behaviour and not referred into safeguarding systems. The case was investigated by the IPCC and it found that the police had failed to act on evidence of the abuse of a vulnerable adult (IPCC, 2008).

Michael Gilbert

Michael was a 26-year-old care leaver with possible mental health problems and was also a heavy cannabis user. He had been serially homeless and was killed by a family who had taken him in and effectively kept him as a slave, tortured him and stolen his welfare benefits for seven years (Flynn, 2011).

David Askew

David lived with his 67-year-old brother and 88-year-old mother. Both brothers had learning disabilities and had suffered hate crimes over many years. David died aged 64 of a heart attack and it was suggested that the stress caused by his experience of the hate crime had exacerbated his heart condition (Tameside Adult Safeguarding Partnership, 2011).

Gemma Hayter

Gemma was murdered by a group of 'friends' at age 27. She lived alone and had a chaotic lifestyle, was prone to exploitation and 'mate' crime (Warwickshire Safeguarding Adults Partnership, 2010).

In addition to these cases concerning individual vulnerable adults, the discussion would be incomplete without reference to the Francis Report and Winterbourne View. Both concerned hospital settings but there is much to be drawn from the review findings in relation to ingrained cultures of abuse and neglect. Both have been mentioned earlier in the text as examples of whistleblowing.

Winterbourne View

Abuse at Winterbourne View private hospital for adults with learning disabilities was drawn to public attention by the BBC's *Panorama* programme (2011). A number of staff were successfully prosecuted under s. 127 Mental Health Act 1983 for ill-treatment and wilful neglect.

The Francis Report

Failures were identified within the Mid Staffordshire NHS Foundation Trust including neglect of patients and failing to respect their dignity. Wards were understaffed and a poor organizational target-driven culture remained largely unchallenged (Francis, 2010).

Learning lessons

At every level, ranging from government statements, researchers and the reports themselves, practitioners are implored to learn the lessons from recommendations of reviews. To translate that call into something tangible it is necessary to consider what should be learnt, by whom and how.

What?

Analysis of serious case reviews has helpfully drawn out key themes and consistent messages, (Manthorpe and Martineau, 2011). This analysis is particularly valuable given the patchy and variable quality of reviews, the difficulty in locating reviews, the range in level of detail and the number of recommendations.

A focused number of achievable recommendations may be ultimately more effective than a detailed lengthy 'wishlist' that may be perceived as daunting, demoralizing and unattainable. Reviews will be most helpful if they take a comprehensive account of the case. As the EHRC noted in its analysis:

> The quality of serious case reviews ... was patchy and they often focus only on the victim and don't consider what contact there had been between the authorities and the perpetrator. The better ones, such as that on Steven Hoskin, have a real value in improving agencies' awareness and understanding of disability-related harassment.
>
> *EHRC, 2011b:136*

The following is a summary of some of the issues often cited in recommendations, many of which actually restate points of recognized good practice:

- follow establish procedures;
- focus on the adult – see the person;
- hold regular case reviews;
- follow up all concerns;
- maintain good practice in recording action and decisions (with reasons);
- provide appropriate support and supervision for staff;
- identify gaps in learning and provide training;
- clarify roles e.g. CQC;
- promote use of whistleblowing;
- provide effective leadership;
- ensure better information-sharing and communication between agencies.

Who?

It is perhaps most important that those agencies with direct involvement in the case and within the ambit of the SAB have the opportunity to learn from the case, with the inevitable benefit of hindsight. To be most effective learning opportunities should reach beyond the local authority to other agencies and include smaller organizations and groups which might encounter similar scenarios whilst not being seen as key players, e.g. domiciliary care agencies. At a local level it is reasonable to expect that any action plan and recommendations should be monitored by the SAB. Given their potential contribution, it is unfortunate that the review of *No Secrets* noted poor participation of general practitioners and mental health trusts (DH, 2009).

If practitioners are to learn from serious case reviews, there needs to be a genuine commitment to appropriate dissemination beyond reliance on media representation of the facts. This entails not only ensuring practitioners have access to the materials, but also that they have time to read and reflect on said findings. Here, it is useful to note that Adult Protection Committees in Scotland issue briefings to practitioners on review findings (Cornish and Preston-Shoot, 2013).

There is also a case for national dissemination. The review of *No Secrets* questioned whether a national database of recommendations from serious case reviews might usefully be established. Unfortunately, although there was some support for this suggestion, notably from the police, it does not feature in the Care Act 2014 or as a policy initiative. Beyond agencies with responsibilities in adult safeguarding, reviews can also contribute to awareness-raising amongst the general public, if reported accurately in the local and national press.

How?

Given the emphasis of recommendations on communication between agencies, ideally learning would take place in a joint forum with opportunities for agencies to share understanding (Aylett, 2008). Inevitably, agencies will be made aware of recommendations that call for changes in practice or for existing procedures to be followed more closely. It is also important that positive examples of changes in practice are highlighted, emphasizing the opportunity that a serious case review can provide to improve and endorse good practice.

Consider the example of Steven Hoskin, whose vulnerability appeared unknown to his landlord. The ECHR reported significant changes in practice by the landlord in collating information about tenants and including a commitment not to send written letters to people with literacy problems.

Further reading

Manthorpe, J and S Martineau, S (2010) 'Serious case reviews in adult safeguarding in England' 41 *British Journal of Social Work* 224 is an analysis of 22 serious case reviews covering rationale for the review, detail of the victim, alleged abuser and setting, type of abuse, process, cost and timescale of the review and its recommendations.

EHRC (2011a) *Hidden in Plain Sight: Inquiry into Disability-related Harassment*: this report includes detail of some of the cases referred to in this chapter, including that of Steven Hoskin.

Critical perspectives of safeguarding boards are provided in:

Braye, S, D Orr and M Preston-Shoot (2012) 'The governance of adult safeguarding: findings from research' 14(2) *Journal of Adult Protection* 55

Reid, D, B Penhale, J Manthorpe, N Perkins, L Pinkney and S Hussein (2009) 'Form and function: views from members of adult protection committees in England and Wales' 11(4) *Journal of Adult Protection* 20–29

8

CONCLUSION: KEY DEVELOPMENTS ACROSS THE UK

This chapter offers some concluding thoughts in relation to the law and safeguarding adults, particularly the case for legislative reform. It also signals some areas of possible further reform relating to corporate neglect and professional regulation. The chapter closes with a table comparing the law reforms in England and Wales with the legislative framework provided by the Adult Support and Protection (Scotland) Act 2007.

It should be clear from reading this text that there is a plethora of legislation that in some way or other has an application to adult safeguarding. It could be argued that further legislation will simply add to this body. Of course, it is not volume that counts, it is the content and purpose of legislation, its clarity and direction. Mandelstam asks 'why there is so much law used to such little effect to protect people at their most vulnerable' (2011a:298)? Here the argument that less is more may apply. That is the stance adopted by the Law Commission in relation to adult social care law generally. The awareness of professionals and willingness to engage with law is also highly significant.

There will undoubtedly continue to be debate about the precise content and likely impact of any legislation. Elements of the new framework have been considered, and there is precedent in the form of the Scottish legislation. Beyond that detail it is also important to think more broadly about the role of legislation. Perhaps here the argument in favour of legislation can be made most forcefully. Legislation represents a clear statement of the value society gives to an issue. To introduce adult protection legislation would not be to say that adult protection is the same as child protection. But it would make a clear statement that society will not tolerate either form of abuse. Indeed, Baroness Hale, responding to the Law Commission consultation remarked:

> Statutory works tend to take priority over softer obligations. It is for this reason that adult safeguarding has been described as a 'poor relation' to child protection. (Law Commission, 2011b)

High standards of professionalism are demanded from those working in social care. The culture of social workers being 'damned if they do, and damned if they don't' is familiar and reinforced with publication of the details of cases which end in tragedy. Legislation will not achieve an end to such cases, or refocus the approach of the media. Action on Elder Abuse acknowledges that:

> Legislation on its own is not the panacea that can guarantee safeguarding in each and every situation. It can only be one option among a range that must include the education of society to alter their perceptions and responses to vulnerability.
> (Fitzgerald, 2008)

It may, however, make for clearer lines of accountability and a more understandable mandate to practise for those currently charged with decision-making in complex, ethically challenging situations in the absence of legal boundaries. On a practical level, the introduction of legislation is often (not always) accompanied by targeted resources for implementation. At the very least, such resources might provide for training of professionals charged with new responsibilities and awareness raising.

Further law reform possibilities

Corporate neglect

As noted in Chapter 3, several staff employed at Winterbourne View hospital were convicted of offences, under the Mental Health Act 1983, of ill-treatment and neglect. Enforcement action was also taken by CQC in respect of the registered person (as discussed in Chapter 5) and the hospital was closed. The argument remains that the company that owned the hospital (and other separate facilities), Castlebeck Ltd, has not been held sufficiently to account for what happened there, described in the serious case review as a 'case study in institutional abuse' (Flynn and Citarella, 2013). A new offence has been proposed as a way of holding corporations to account for their practices and procedures which cause abuse. This proposed reform has been championed by Paul Burstow, MP and former Care Minister. A new section, entitled 'Corporate neglect', was debated in Parliament but not included in the final Care Act 2014:

> A corporate body delivering services covered by sections 8 and 9 of the Act are guilty of an offence if the way in which its activities are managed or organised by its board or senior management neglects or is a substantial element in the existence and or possibility of abuse or neglect occurring.
>
> *Burstow, 2013:203*

Professional regulation

A further area of possible law reform has emerged from the work of the Law Commission (2012). In a tripartite review with the Law Commissions of Scotland and Northern Ireland, the Law Commission has undertaken a review of the regulatory framework governing health and social care professionals. There are currently nine different bodies regulating health professionals and one body regulating social workers. The Law Commission aim is 'to modernise and simplify current arrangements for professional regulation so that all healthcare professionals and social workers in England are subject to the same framework'. A draft Bill has been published.

Data sharing

The Law Commission is also engaged in a consultation on data sharing between public bodies. It notes that:

> There are reported to be significant obstacles to effective data sharing. It is not, however, clear whether these obstacles are the result of inadequacies in the legal regime governing data sharing or the result of a number of practical or cultural barriers. (Law Commission, 2013:1.1)

Recommendations as to law reform in this area will have an impact on safeguarding practice and the sharing of information between, for example, health services and social services.

Safeguarding adults in England, Scotland and Wales

Provisions of the Care Act 2014 have been integrated into the text where relevant as an indication of how the law will change when implemented. This final section includes a brief consideration of the existing statutory framework in Scotland and the new legislation in Wales.

The Adult Support and Protection (Scotland) Act 2007.

The Act introduced new adult protection powers and procedures and established a statutory requirement for multi-agency Adult Protection Committees. Its essential aims were to strengthen measures to give greater protection for those at risk from harm and to improve inter-agency cooperation and the promotion of good interdisciplinary practice in this area of practice.

Social Services and Well-being (Wales) Act 2014

The Welsh Assembly Government commissioned the Welsh Institute for Health and Social Care to review *In Safe Hands* (National Assembly for Wales, 2000), the equivalent guidance to England's *No Secrets* (DH, 2000b). The review was prompted by 'Changes in demographics, significant legislative and regulatory change, policy developments and lessons learnt over the nine years since publication' (Welsh Institute for Health and Social Care, 2010). It found that, whilst *In Safe Hands* had a significant impact on developing arrangements for safeguarding adults in Wales, the original document was currently insufficiently robust, only partially effective and no longer appropriate. Recommendation 2 of 16 reads:

> New legislation is required. The symbolism of legislation is important in fostering cultural change. Safeguarding adults at risk from abuse who cannot protect their own interests must have the same legislative status and priority as protecting children.
> (National Assembly for Wales, 2000)

Key recommendations have been taken forward in the Social Services and Well-being (Wales) Act 2014 as part of an ambitious new framework consolidating arrangements for protection of children and adults.

Provisions from the Scottish, English and Welsh legislation are presented in Table 8.1 (see pages 158–59) which allows for simple comparison of approach.

The table summarizes and simplifies key elements of the Adult Support and Protection (Scotland) Act 2007, Care Act 2014 and the Social Services and Well-being (Wales) Act 2014. At a glance it identifies consistency in some respects but also highlights areas of difference. A few observations may be made, noting, however, that at the time of writing the English and Welsh legislation is not implemented.

Only the Scottish legislation is specifically focused on adult protection. In England and Wales adult protection measures are contained within legislation that has a much broader remit. In England the legislation addresses the whole of adult social care and presents the opportunity to reform and replace a volume of legislation from 1948 onwards. In Wales the new legislation is even more ambitious and wide-ranging, covering all functions of social services and combining law relating to children and adults in one statute. A possible consequence in each case may be that the adult safeguarding measures receive a less focused level of scrutiny and attention.

To whom do the provisions apply? Respondents to the *No Secrets* review were critical of the term 'vulnerable adult' and its link to community care services (DH, 2009). Whilst some people eligible for community care services may also be vulnerable to abuse, there will equally be adults who do not qualify for services but are still vulnerable to abuse. This element of the definition perpetuates a 'welfarist approach to abuse' (Williams, 2008). The preferred term to emerge from the *No Secrets* consultation was 'adult at risk', which features in the Scottish legislation. The Welsh Act also refers to an adult at risk. Underpinning criteria for an adult at risk are set out and the same terms are used to refer to an adult to whom the Act applies but absent the reference to 'at risk'. In a section on the scope of safeguarding, the government acknowledges concerns that the term 'vulnerable adult' may be considered pejorative but rejects the Law Commission's suggested term of 'adult at risk' as potentially too broad and, indeed, any other term arguing that 'the use of any particular descriptive term in the legislation will be problematic and unlikely to be future-proof or suitable for a modern care and support statute' (DH, 2009). Instead the stated position is to emphasize the underpinning criteria. Such reluctance to engage with the question of definition is not helpful for practitioners who are likely to neither refer to the full criteria nor simply to 'adults' and may revert to the familiar but contested term 'vulnerable adult' or, in practice, adopt the term 'adult at risk'.

'Harm' is used in the Adult Support and Protection (Scotland) Act 2007 and is open to broad interpretation. Indeed, the Code of Practice accompanying the Act states further that 'No category of harm is excluded simply because it is not explicitly listed ... Also what constitutes serious harm will be different for different persons.' (Scottish Government, 2009:13) 'Harm' as advocated by the Law Commission was rejected, both Acts favouring 'abuse and neglect'. Familiar categories of physical, sexual, psychological, emotional or financial abuse are cited in the Welsh Act and whilst initially it appeared that a drafting error in the English Bill omitted any reference to types of abuse other than financial, the final Act confirms that financial abuse is the only type of abuse or neglect which merits further definition. In either case the wording in the Adult Support and Protection (Scotland) Act 2007 to 'all harmful conduct' followed by examples is preferable as it allows flexibly for inclusion of the possibility of expanding knowledge of types of harm.

In relation to governance, *No Secrets* (DH, 2000b) anticipated a role for safeguarding boards, but, unsurprisingly, in the absence of a statutory

	Adult Support and Protection (Scotland) Act 2007	Care Act 2014 (England)	Social Services and Well-being (Wales) Act 2014
Application to subject	Adult at risk: (a) are unable to safeguard their own well-being, property, rights or other interests, (b) are at risk of harm, and (c) because they are affected by disability, mental disorder, illness or physical or mental infirmity, are more vulnerable to being harmed than adults who are not so affected. (s. 3(1))	An adult who: (a) has needs for care and support (whether or not the authority is meeting any of those needs), (b) is experiencing, or is at risk of, abuse or neglect, and (c) as a result of those needs is unable to protect himself or herself against the abuse or neglect or the risk of it. (s. 42(1))	An 'adult at risk' is an adult who— (a) is experiencing or is at risk of abuse or neglect, (b) has needs for care and support (whether or not the authority is meeting any of those needs), and (c) as a result of those needs is unable to protect himself or herself against the abuse or neglect or the risk of it. (s. 126(1))
'Abuse'	'Harm' includes all harmful conduct, in particular – physical harm, psychological harm (e.g. causing fear, alarm or distress), unlawful conduct which appropriates or adversely affects property, rights or interests, conduct which causes self-harm. (s. 53(1))	Abuse and neglect: 'Abuse' includes – (a) having money or other property stolen, (b) being defrauded, (c) being put under pressure in relation to money or other property, (d) having money or other property misused. (s. 42(3))	Abuse and neglect: Abuse means physical, sexual, psychological, emotional or financial abuse, and financial abuse includes— (a) having money or other property stolen, (b) being defrauded; (c) being put under pressure in relation to money or other property, (d) having money or other property misused. (s. 197)
Duty to investigate	A council must make inquiries about a person's well-being, property or financial affairs if it knows or believes a) that the person is an adult at risk and b) that it might need to intervene to protect the person's well-being, property or financial affairs. (s. 4)	A local authority with reasonable cause to suspect that an adult in its area – (meets criteria above) it must make (or cause to be made) enquiries to enable it to decide whether any action should be taken and if so, what and by whom. (s. 42(1)(2)	If a local authority has reasonable cause to suspect that a person within its area is an adult at risk, it must make (or cause to be made) whatever enquiries it thinks necessary to enable it to decide whether any action should be taken and, if so, what and by whom. (s. 126(2))

Governance	Each council must establish an 'Adult Protection Committee'. (s. 42)	Each local authority must establish a Safeguarding Adults Board. (s. 43)	Each authority (s. 134) must establish a Safeguarding Adults Board accountable to a National Independent Safeguarding Board. (s. 132)
Information sharing/ cooperation	Public bodies (listed) must cooperate with a council making inquiries and each other. (s. 5)	Local authority and its relevant partners (listed) (and others considered appropriate) must co-operate in their functions relating to adults with needs for care and support. (s. 6)	Relevant partners have a duty to co-operate and provide information to the local authority to assist with the exercise of any social services functions (s. 164).
Mandatory reporting	Where a public body/office-holder knows or believes an adult is at risk and action needs to be taken to protect the person from harm – must report the case to the council (s. 5(3))	No provision	If a relevant partner of a local authority has reasonable cause to suspect that a person is an adult at risk and appears to be within the authority's area, it must inform the local authority of that fact. (s. 128)
Right of entry	Council officer may enter any place to decide whether it needs to do anything to protect an adult at risk from harm. (s. 7(1))	Rejected in separate consultation	With police constable via adult protection and support order to ascertain if the person is making decisions freely, and to assess whether the person is at risk. (s. 126(3))
Powers	Right to interview in private (s. 8), conduct a medical examination (s. 9), and examine records (s. 10)	Rejected in separate consultation	Right to interview in private (s. 127 (2)(a))
Orders	Assessment orders (s. 11), removal orders (s. 14), and banning orders (s. 19)	No available orders	Adult protection and support order (s. 127)

Table 8.1: Provisions from the Scottish, English and Welsh legislation

requirement, practices were inconsistent and, where boards were established, membership varied (Perkins et al., 2007). In their work on governance of adult safeguarding, Braye et al. argue that:

> Specific legislation that sets out for Safeguarding Boards roles and functions would help to standardise policy and procedures, to hold agencies more easily accountable, to clarify responsibilities and to ensure participation, in ways that guidance, differentially binding on the partners, has not so far been able to do. (2011c)

Boards will be statutorily required across all three jurisdictions when the English Act and Welsh Act are implemented. It is notable that only the Welsh Bill incorporates a level of accountability to a National Board.

Collaborative work is essential to secure a timely and coordinated response to safeguarding concerns. Regrettably, as discussed in Chapter 7, lack of or ineffective sharing of information has been a feature of both child and adult serious case reviews. It is encouraging to see a duty to cooperate in each framework and to hope this will strengthen inter-agency working within a framework of accountability to the board.

The final section of the table reveals least consensus. Whilst the Adult Support and Protection (Scotland) Act 2007 includes a range of orders and the Welsh Act includes provision for entry and assessment, the English Act remains silent on any powers to support the duty to investigate or take subsequent action. The government response to the separate consultation relating to a power of entry concluded that it is not necessary (DH, 2013). This is perhaps the most disappointing omission from the Care Act 2014 given that early assessment of practice in Scotland would not suggest that the existence of greater powers necessarily leads to excessive intervention, and when exercised in accordance with guiding principles and the Human Rights Act 1998 may provide those working in safeguarding with positive options (Preston-Shoot and Cornish, 2014).

It has been a long journey but some form of safeguarding legislation now exists in England, Wales and Scotland and it is perhaps inevitable, because of devolution for Scotland and Wales, that there will be some differences in the precise detail of the law. Given that abuse of adults occurs across the UK, differing levels of protection across borders for adults who suffer abuse presents an ongoing challenge to good practice in safeguarding.

Further reading

The following sources include discussion of the Scottish legislation and its operation.

Calder, B (2010) *A Guide to the Adult Support and Protection (Scotland) Act 2007*

Keenan, T (2011) *Crossing the Acts: The Support and Protection of Adults at Risk with Mental Disorder across the Scottish Legislative Frameworks*

Patrick, H and N Smith (2009) *Adult Protection and the Law in Scotland*

Preston-Shoot, M and S Cornish (2014) 'Paternalism or proportionality? Experiences and outcomes of the Adult Support and Protection (Scotland) Act 2007' 16(1) *Journal of Adult Protection* 17

USEFUL WEBSITES

www.ageuk.org.uk
A campaigning organisation on age-related issues with excellent factsheets.

www.carersuk.org.uk
A campaigning, research-active national charity to support carers.

www.cps.gov.uk
The Crown Prosecution Service website with links to the prosecution codes.

www.cqc.org.uk
The Care Quality Commission.

www.elderabuse.org.uk
Action on Elder Abuse, a pressure group that provides useful and up-to-date information and a newsletter.

www.gov.uk/forced-marriage
Forced Marriage Unit – information for professionals supporting and advising on forced marriage.

www.hcpc-uk.org
The Health and Care Professionals Council website, including the register of social workers.

www.justice.gov.uk/victims-and-witnesses/cica
For details of the Criminal Injuries Compensation Scheme.

www.lgo.org.uk
The website of the Local Government Ombudsman with information on how to make a complaint and details of its investigations.

www.parliament.gov.uk
Track the progress of Bills through the parliamentary process on the Parliament site.

www.pasauk.org.uk
The Practitioner Alliance for Safeguarding Adults.

www.pcaw.co.uk
Public Concern at Work – the independent body that provides support and advice to whistleblowers.

www.scie.org.uk
The Social Care Institute for Excellence produces a range of research publications, knowledge reviews and e-learning materials relevant to safeguarding.

www.voiceyp.org.uk
Getting young voices heard and empowering young people.

www.womensaid.org
Women's Aid.

GLOSSARY

Alert
The initial contact to a safeguarding authority raising a concern about possible abuse.

Appropriate adult
An individual who will accompany a vulnerable adult suspect in a police interview.

Best interests
The principle which guides acts taken and decision-making for an adult who lacks capacity.

Court of Protection
The specialist court for matters relating to mental capacity.

Data protection
Processing information about individuals safely and in compliance with the principles of the Data Protection Act 1998.

Declaration
An order from the Court of Protection declaring legal action.

Deprivation of Liberty Safeguards
A procedure to safeguard the interests of a person who lacks capacity to consent to arrangements which amount to continuous supervision and control and which he or she is not free to leave.

Deputy
A person appointed by the Court of Protection to make ongoing decisions for a person lacking capacity.

Disclosure and Barring Service
The body responsible for ensuring an unsuitable person does not work with vulnerable adults.

Duty
A mandatory obligation imposed on a local authority by statute, often indicated by the word 'shall' or 'must'.

Eligibility criteria
A structured way of allocating limited resources to individuals with identified needs.

Independent Mental Capacity Advocate
An advocate appointed to represent and support an adult who lacks capacity when making specified decisions.

Inherent jurisdiction
Powers exercisable in the High Court in relation to adults lacking capacity prior to the introduction of the MCA 2005. The jurisdiction continues to apply in respect of adults who have capacity within the meaning of the MCA 2005 but are nevertheless considered vulnerable.

Lasting power of attorney
A document used when an individual with capacity (the donor) wishes to appoint a person(s) (the donee) to make welfare and/or financial decisions on their behalf, on loss of capacity.

Law Commission
An independent body of lawyers whose role is to make recommendations for the reform and consolidation of specific areas of law.

Liability
To be legally responsible for an action.

Managing authority
The body (care homes and hospitals) which can apply for a deprivation of liberty authorization.

Official Solicitor
A role within the MoJ providing representation for incapacitated adults when there is no one else available or suitable to act.

Personal assistant
An individual employed directly by a person in receipt of direct payments.

Power
Where a local authority has a legal discretion to act, often indicated by the word 'may'.

Proportionality
Responding in a way that balances risk and is the least intrusive way of achieving an objective.

Referral
When an alert/concern meets local safeguarding thresholds (where these exist) and an investigation proceeds.

Safeguarding Adults Boards
A multi-agency board which coordinates safeguarding adults practice in a geographical area.

Serious case review
A review of practice following the death of a vulnerable adult with a view to learning lessons for the future, to be replaced by Safeguarding Adults Reviews under the Care Act 2014.

Special measures
Measures introduced to assist vulnerable witnesses to give their best evidence to a court e.g. use of an intermediary.

Supervisory body
The body (local authorities) which receives and may grant or refuse applications for a deprivation of liberty authorization.

BIBLIOGRAPHY

Action on Elder Abuse (1994) *Newsletter* (London: Age Concern)

Action on Elder Abuse (2000) *The Great Taboo: Sexual Abuse of Older People* Working Paper No 5 (London: Action on Elder Abuse)

Action on Elder Abuse (2004) *Hidden Voices: Older People's Experience of Abuse* (London: Help the Aged)

Action on Elder Abuse (no date) *Working Together: A Guide to Safely Recruiting and Working with Personal Assistants* (booklet and DVD) www.elderabuse.org.uk

ADASS (2011) *Carers and Safeguarding Adults: Working Together to Improve Outcomes* (London: ADSS)

ADASS and LGA (2013a) *Adult Safeguarding and Domestic Abuse: A Guide to Support Practitioners and Managers* (London: ADASS/LGA)

ADASS and LGA (2013b) *Safeguarding Adults: Advice and Guidance to Directors of Adult Social Services* (London: ADASS/LGA)

ADSS (2005) *Safeguarding Adults: A National Framework of Standards for Good Practice and Outcomes in Adult Protection Work* (London: ADSS)

ADSS (2006) (updated 2010) *Vulnerable Adult Serious Case Review Guidance: Developing a Local Protocol* (London: ADSS)

Alzheimer's Society (2013) *Low Expectations: Attitudes on Choice, Care and Community for People with Dementia in Care Homes* (London: Alzheimer's Society)

Ashton DJ, G (2012) *Mental Capacity: Law and Practice* 2nd edn (Bristol: Jordans)

Aylett, J (2008) 'Learning the lessons in training from abuse inquiries: findings and recommendations' 10(4) *Journal of Adult Protection* 7

Ball, C (2014) *Looked After Children* (Basingstoke: Palgrave Macmillan)

BASW (2012) *The Code of Ethics for Social Work* (Birmingham: London)

BBC *Panorama* (2011) 'Undercover care: the abuse exposed (Winterbourne View)' broadcast 31 May 2011

Brammer, A (2001) 'Elder abuse' in L A Cull and J Roche (eds), *The Law and Social Work: Contemporary Issues for Practice* (Basingstoke: Palgrave Macmillan)

Brammer, A (2010) *Social Work Law* (Harlow: Pearson)

Brammer, A (2012) 'Inside the Court of Protection' 14(6) *Journal of Adult Protection* 297

Brammer, A (2014) 'Carers and the Mental Capacity Act 2005' *Criminal Law Review* (forthcoming)

Braye, S, D Orr and M Preston-Shoot (2011a) 'Conceptualising and responding to self-neglect: the challenges for adult safeguarding' 13(4) *Journal of Adult Protection* 182–93

Braye, S, D Orr and M Preston-Shoot (2011b) *Self-neglect and Adult Safeguarding: Findings from Research* (London: SCIE)

Braye, S, D Orr and M Preston-Shoot (2011c) *The Governance of Adult Safeguarding: Findings from Research into Safeguarding Adults Boards: Final Report to the Department of Health* (London: SCIE)

Braye, S, D Orr and M Preston-Shoot (2012) 'The governance of adult safeguarding: findings from research' 14(2) *Journal of Adult Protection* 55

Brown, H (2012) 'Not only a crime but a tragedy [...] exploring the murder of adults with disabilities by their parents' 14(1) *Journal of Adult Protection* 6

Brown, R (2009) *The Approved Mental Health Professional's Guide to Mental Health Law* 2nd edn (Exeter: Learning Matters)

Brown, H, J Stein and V Turk (1995) 'The sexual abuse of adults with learning disabilities: report of a second two-year incidence survey' 8 *Mental Handicap Research* 3–24

Bruder, C and B S Kroese (2005) 'The efficacy of interventions designed to prevent and protect people with intellectual disabilities from sexual abuse: a review of the literature' 7(2) *Journal of Adult Protection* 13

Burstow, P (2013) 'Care and corporate neglect: the case for action' 15(4) *Journal of Adult Protection* 203

Butler, J (2012) *Community Care Law and Local Authority Handbook* 2nd edn (Bristol: Jordans)

Cairns, R, P Brown, H Grant-Peterkin, G Owen, G Richardson, G Szmukler and M Hotopf (2011) 'Mired in confusion: making sense of the Deprivation of Liberty Safeguards' 51 *Medicine, Science and the Law* 228

Calder, B (2010) *A Guide to the Adult Support and Protection (Scotland) Act 2007* (Dundee: Dundee University Press)

Cambridge, P and S Carnaby (2000) 'A personal touch: managing the risks of abuse during intimate and personal care' 2(4) *Journal of Adult Protection* 4

Carers UK (2013) *The State of Caring 2013* (London: Carers UK)

Carr, H (2012) 'Rational men and difficult women – *R (on the application of McDonald) v Royal Borough of Kensington and Chelsea* [2011] UKSC 33' 34(2) *Journal of Social Welfare and Family law* 219

Clapton, K (2013) 'Developing professional boundaries guidance for social workers' 15(1) *Journal of Adult Protection* 37

Clements, L (2005) *Carers and the Law* (London, Carers UK)

Clements, L (2011a) *Carers and their Rights: The Law Relating to Carers* (London: Carers UK)

Clements, L (2011b) 'Disability, dignity and cri de coeur' 6 *European Human Rights Law Review* 675

Clements, L (2011c) 'Social care developments: a sideways look at personalisation and tightening eligibility criteria' 1 *Elder Law Journal* 47

Clements, L and C Thompson (2011) *Community Care and the Law* 5th edn (London: Legal Action Group)

Commission for Social Care Inspection (2008) *Safeguarding Adults: A Study of the Effectiveness of Arrangements to Safeguard Adults from Abuse* (London: CSCI)

Cooper, C, A Selwood and G Livingston (2008) 'The prevalence of elder abuse and neglect: a systematic review' 37(2) *Age and Ageing* 151

Cooper, P (2014) *Court and Legal Skills* (Basingstoke: Palgrave Macmillan)

Cornish, S and M Preston-Shoot (2013) 'Governance in adult safeguarding in Scotland since the implementation of the Adult Support and Protection (Scotland) Act 2007' 15(5) *Journal of Adult Protection* 223

CPS (2007) *Policy for Prosecuting Cases of Disability Hate Crime* (London: CPS)

CPS (2008) *Prosecuting Crimes against Older People* (London: CPS)

CQC (2013a) *Enforcement Policy* (London CQC)

CQC (2013b) *Not Just a Number: Home Care Inspection Programme* (London: CQC)

CQC (2013c) *Our Safeguarding Protocol: The Care Quality Commission's Responsibility and Commitment to Safeguarding* (London: CQC)

CQC (2013d) *Raising Standards: Putting People First* (London: CQC)

Davies, M (ed.) (2012) *Social Work with Adults* (Basingstoke: Palgrave Macmillan)

DCA (2007) *Mental Capacity Act 2005 Code of Practice* (London: TSO)

DCSF (2009) *Forced Marriage: Prevalence and Service Response* (London: National Centre for Social Research/DCSF)

DH (2000a) *Data Protection Act 1998: Guidance to Social Services* (London: DH)

DH (2000b) *No Secrets: Guidance on Developing and Implementing Multi-agency Policies and Procedures to Protect Vulnerable Adults from Abuse* (London: DH)

DH (2003) *Fair Access to Care Services* LAC 2003/12 (London: DH)

DH (2008a) *Safeguarding Adults: A Review of the 'No Secrets' Guidance* (London: DH)

DH (2008b) *Transforming Adult Social Care* LAC 2008 (London: DH)

DH (2009a) *Code of Practice to the Mental Health Act 1983* (Norwich: TSO)

DH (2009b) *Safeguarding Adults: Report on the Consultation on the Review of No Secrets – Guidance on Developing and Implementing Multi-agency Policies and Procedures to Protect Vulnerable Adults from Abuse* (London: TSO)

DH (2010a) *Practical Approaches to Safeguarding and Personalisation* (London: DH)

DH (2010b) *Prioritising Need in the Context of Putting People First: A Whole Systems Approach to Eligibility for Adult Social Care* (London: DH)

DH (2010c) *The Vision for Adult Social Care* (DH: London)

DH (2011a) *Framework for Supporting Personal Assistants Working in Adult Social Care* (London: DH)

DH (2011b) 'Statement of government policy on adult safeguarding' (London: DH)

DH (2012) *Consultation on New Safeguarding Power* (London: DH)

DH (2013) *Government Response to the Safeguarding Power of Entry Consultation* (London: DH)

DH and Social Services Inspectorate (1993) *No Longer Afraid: The Safeguarding of Older People in Domestic Settings* (London: HMSO)

EHRC (2011a) *Close to Home: An Inquiry into Older People and Human Rights in Home Care* (London: EHRC)

EHRC (2011b) *Hidden in Plain Sight: Inquiry into Disability-related Harassment* (London: EHRC)

Ellis, K (2004) 'Promoting rights or avoiding litigation? The introduction of the Human Rights Act 1998 into adult social care in England' 7(3) *European Journal of Social Work* 321

Ferguson, I (2007) 'Increasing user choice or privatising risk? The antinomies of personalisation' 37(3) *British Journal of Social Work* 387

Fitzgerald, G (2008) 'No secrets, safeguarding adults and adult protection' in J Pritchard (ed.), *Good Practice in Safeguarding Adults: Working Effectively in Adult Protection* (London: Jessica Kingsley)

Flynn, M (2005) *Developing the Role for Personal Assistants* (Leeds: Skills for Care)

Flynn, M (2007) *The Murder of Steven Hoskin: A Serious Case Review – Executive Summary* (Truro: Cornwall Adult Protection Committee)

Flynn, M (2010) *Serious Case Review: Ann* www.sheffield.gov.uk/caresupport/adult/adult-abuse/partnership/serious-case-reviews.html

Flynn, M (2011) *The Murder of Adult A (Michael Gilbert): A Serious Case Review* (Luton: Luton Safeguarding Vulnerable Adults Board)

Flynn, M and H Brown (2010) 'Safeguarding adults with learning disabilities against abuse' in G Grant et al. (eds), *Learning Disability: A Life Cycle Approach* 2nd edn (Maidenhead: McGraw-Hill)

Flynn, M and V Citarella (2012) *Winterbourne View Hospital: A Serious Case Review* (Bristol: South Gloucestershire Council on Behalf of South Gloucestershire Safeguarding Adults Board)

Flynn, M and V Citarella (2013) 'Winterbourne View Hospital: a glimpse of the legacy' 15(4) *Journal of Adult Protection* 173

Francis, R (2010) *The Independent Inquiry into Care Provided by Mid-Staffordshire NHS Foundation Trust 2005–2009* (London: DH)

Francis, R (2013) *Report of the Mid Staffordshire NHS Foundation Trust Public Inquiry* (London: TSO)

George, R H (2011) 'In defence of dissent: *R (McDonald) v Royal Borough of Kensington and Chelsea*' 1(4) *Elder Law Journal*

Gilhooly, M, D Cairns, M Davies, P Harries, J Gilhoolu and E Notley (2013) 'Framing the detection of financial elder abuse as bystander intervention: decision cues, pathways to detection and barriers to action' 15(2) *Journal of Adult Protection* 54

Hartley-Jones, P (2011) 'The role of the Office of the Public Guardian in investigations of abuse' 13(3) *Journal of Adult Protection* 160

HCPC (2008) *Standards of Conduct, Performance and Ethics* (London: HCPC) www.hcpc-uk/org

HCPC (2012) *Standards of Proficiency: Social Workers in England* (London: HCPC)

HSCIC (2013) *Mental Capacity Act 2005, Deprivation of Liberty Safeguards Assessments (England) Annual Report 2012/13* (London: HSCIC)

Herring, J (2009) *Older People in Law and Society* (Oxford: Oxford University Press)

Herring, J (2013) *Caring and the Law* (Oxford: Hart Publishing)

Hewitt, D (2012) 'Objection, purpose and normality: three ways in which the courts have inhibited safeguarding' 14(6) *Journal of Adult Protection* 280

HM Government (2008) *Information Sharing: Guidance for Practitioners and Managers* (London: DCSF)

HM Government (2013) *Working Together to Safeguard Children: A Guide to Inter-agency Working to Safeguard and Promote the Welfare of Children* (London HM Government)

Hobbs, A and A Alonzi (2013) 'Mediation and family group conferences in adult safeguarding' 15(2) *Journal of Adult Protection* 69

Hollomotz, A (2011) *Learning Difficulties and Sexual Vulnerability* (London: Jessica Kingsley)

Home Office (1999) *Caring for Young People and the Vulnerable? Guidance on Preventing Abuse of Trust* (London: Home Office)

Home Office (2012) *Cross-Government Definition of Domestic Violence: A Consultation – Summary of Responses* (London: Home Office)

Horsey, K and E Rackley (2013) *Tort Law* (Oxford: Oxford University Press)

Hussein, S et al. (2009) 'Accusations of misconduct amongst staff working with vulnerable adults in England' 31(1) *Journal of Social Welfare and Family Law* 17

IPCC (2009) *Report into the Contact Between Fiona Pilkington and Leicestershire Constabulary 2004–2007* (Manchester: IPCC)

Jeary, K (2004) 'Sexual abuse of elderly people: would we rather not know the details?' 6 *Journal of Adult Protection* 21

Johns, R (2014) *Capacity and Autonomy* (Basingstoke: Palgrave Macmillan)

Judicial College (2013) *Equal Treatment Bench Book* www judiciary.gov.uk

Judiciary of England and Wales (2011) *Court of Protection Report 2010* (London: Judiciary of England and Wales)

Kalaga, H and P Kingston (2007) *A Review of Literature on Effective Interventions that Prevent and Respond to Harm against Adults* (Edinburgh: Scottish Government Social Research)

Kazimirski, A, P Keogh, V Kumari, R Smith, S Gowland, S Purdon and N Khanum (2008) *The Right to Choose: Multi-agency Statutory Guidance for Dealing with Forced Marriage* (London: FMU)

Keenan, T (2011) *Crossing the Acts: The Support and Protection of Adults at Risk with Mental Disorder across the Scottish Legislative Frameworks* (Birmingham: BASW)

Kline, R and M Preston-Shoot (2012) *Professional Accountability in Social care and Health: Challenging Unacceptable Practice and its Management* (Exeter: Learning Matters)

Law Commission (2008) *Adult Social Care: Scoping Report* (London: Law Commission)

Law Commission (2010) *Adult Social Care* Consultation Paper No 192 (London: Law Commission)

Law Commission (2011a) *Adult Social Care* Law Com No 326 (London: Law Commission)

Law Commission (2011b) *Adult Social Care Consultation: Analysis* (London: Law Commission)

Law Commission (2012) *Consumer Redress for Misleading and Aggressive Practices* Law Com No 332, Scottish Law Commission No 226 (Law Commission/Scottish Law Commission)

Law Commission (2013) *Data Sharing between Public Bodies* Consultation paper 214 (London: Law Commission)

Mandelstam, M (2011a) *How We Treat the Sick: Neglect and Abuse in our Health Services* (London: Jessica Kingsley)

Mandelstam, M (2011b) *Safeguarding Adults at Risk of Harm: A Legal Guide for Practitioners* Adults Services SCIE Report 50 (London: SCIE)

Mandelstam, M (2013) *Safeguarding Adults and the Law* 2nd edn (London: Jessica Kingsley)

Mantell, A and T Scraggs (2011) *Safeguarding Adults in Social Work* (London: Learning Matters)

Manthorpe, J and S Martineau (2010) 'Serious case reviews in adult safeguarding in England' 41 *British Journal of Social Work* 224

Marsland, D, P Oakes and C White (2007) 'Abuse in care? The identification of early indicators of the abuse of people with learning disabilities in residential settings' 9(4) *Journal of Adult Protection* 6

McDonald, A (2010) 'The impact of the 2005 Mental Capacity Act on social workers' decision making and approaches to the assessment of risk' 40 *British Journal of Social Work* 1229

McGregor, K (2012) 'Winterbourne View care staff jailed for abuse' www.communitycare.co.uk/2012/10/26/winterbourne-view-care-staff-jailed-for-abuse

McKeough, C (2009) 'Reflections and learning from adult protection policy in Kent and Medway' 11(1) *Journal of Adult Protection* 9

McKeough, C and E Knell-Taylor (2002) 'Protecting vulnerable adults where they may be both victim and perpetrator' 4(4) *Journal of Adult Protection* 10

McLaughlin, K (2010) 'The social worker versus the General Social Care Council: an analysis of Care Standards Tribunal hearings and decisions' 40 *British Journal of Social Work* 311

Minister of State (2010) *Government Response to the Consultation on Safeguarding Adults: The Review of the No Secrets Guidance* (London: DH)

MoJ (2008) *Deprivation of Liberty Safeguards: Code of Practice to Supplement the Mental Capacity Act 2005 Code of Practice* (Norwich: TSO)

MoJ (2009) *Forced Marriage (Civil Protection) Act 2007 Guidance for Local Authorities and Relevant Third Party and Information Relating to Multi-agency Partnership Working* (London: MoJ)

MoJ (2011) *Achieving Best Evidence in Criminal Proceedings: Guidance on Interviewing Victims and Witnesses, and Guidance on Using Special Measures* (London: MoJ)

MoJ (2012) *The Criminal Injuries Compensation Scheme 2012* (London: TSO)

MoJ (2013) *Code of Practice for Victims of Crime* (London: TSO)

Munby, Sir James (2011) 'Dignity happiness and human rights' 1(1) *Elder Law Journal* 32

Munby, Sir James (2014) *Transparency in the Court of Protection: Publication of Judgments – Practice Guidance*, issued on 16 January 2014 by the President of the Court of Protection www.judiciary.gov.uk/Resources/JCO/Documents/Guidance/transparency-in-the-cop.pdf

Mustafa, N (2008) 'How the United Kingdom's Criminal Records Bureau can reduced the prevalence of elder abuse by improving recruitment decision-making' 10(4) *Journal of Adult Protection* 37

National Assembly for Wales (2000) *In Safe Hands: Implementing Adult Protection Procedures in Wales* (Cardiff: National Assembly for Wales)

NPIA (2011) *Guidance on Safeguarding and Investigating the Abuse of Vulnerable Adults* 1st edn (London: NPIA)

O'Keeffe, M, A Hills, M Doyle, C McCreadie, S Scholes, R Constantine, A Tinker, J Manthorpe, S Biggs and B Erens (2007) *UK Study of Abuse and Neglect of Older People: Prevalence Survey Report* (London: National Centre for Social Research)

OPG (2013) *Safeguarding Policy* (London: OPG)

Parry, I (2013) 'Adult safeguarding and the role of housing' 1 *Journal of Adult Protection* 15

Patrick, H and N Smith (2009) *Adult Protection and the Law in Scotland* (London: Bloomsbury Professional)

PCAW and University of Greenwich (2013) *Whistleblowing: The Inside Story* (London: PCAW)

Penhale, B and J Parker (2007) *Working with Vulnerable Adults* (The Social Work Skills Series) (London: Routledge)

Perkins, N, B Penhale, D Reid and L Pinkney (2007) 'Partnership means protection? Perceptions of the effectiveness of multi-agency working and the regulatory framework within adult protection in England and Wales' 9(3) *Journal of Adult Protection* 9

Phelan, A (2013) (ed.) *International Perspectives on Elder Abuse* (London: Routledge)

Pinkney, L, B Penhale, J Manthorpe, N Perkins, D Reid and S Hussein (2008) 'Voices from the frontline: social work practitioners' perceptions of multi-agency working in adult protection in England and Wales' 10(4) *Journal of Adult Protection* 12–23

Plotnikoff, J and R Woolfson (2008) 'Making best use of the intermediary special measure at trial' 2 *Criminal Law Review* 91

Police and Criminal Evidence Act 1984 (2012) *Code C: The Code of Practice for the Detention, Treatment and Questioning of Persons by Police Officers* (London: TSO)

Preston-Shoot, M and S Cornish (2014) 'Paternalism or proportionality? Experiences and outcomes of the Adult Support and Protection (Scotland) Act 2007' 16(1) *Journal of Adult Protection* 5

Pritchard, J (ed.) (2009) *Good Practice in the Law and Safeguarding Adults: Criminal Justice and Adult Protection* (London: Jessica Kingsley)

Pritchard, J and S Leslie (2011) *Recording Skills in Safeguarding Adults; Best Practice and Evidential Requirements* (London: Jessica Kingsley)

Qureshi, H and M McNay (2011) *Social Care Workforce Research Initiative* (London: Social Care Workforce Research Unit)

Redley, M, I Claire, M Dunn, M Platten and A Holland (2011) 'Introducing the Mental Capacity Advocate (IMCA) Service and the reform of adult safeguarding procedures' 41 *British Journal of Social Work* 1058

Rosenbach, A (2011) *Internal Management Review of the Regulation of Winterbourne View* (London: CQC)

SCIE (2011) *Prevention in Adult Safeguarding* Adult Services Report 41 (London: SCIE)

Scottish Government (2009) *Adults Support and Protection Act 2007 Code of Practice* (Edinburgh: Scottish Government)

Scourfield, P (2010) 'Reflections on the serious case review of a female adult (JK)' 12(4) *Journal of Adult Protection* 16

Seddon, D, C Robinson, C Reeves, Y Tommis, B Woods and I Russel (2007) 'In their own rights: translating the policy of carers assessments into practice' 37 *British Journal of Social Work* 1335

Spencer-Lane, T (2011) 'Reforming the legal framework for adult safeguarding: the Law Commission's final recommendations on adult social care' 13(5) *Journal of Adult Protection* 275

Surrey Safeguarding Adults Board (2013) *A Serious Case Review. The Death of Mrs Gloria Foster* www.surreycc.gov.uk

Sutherland, K and S Leatherman (2006) *Regulation and Quality Improvement: A Review of the Evidence* (London: Health Foundation)

Tameside Adult Safeguarding Partnership (2011) *Executive Summary of the Serious Case Review in Respect of Adult A* (Tameside: Tameside Adult Safeguarding Partnership)

The College of Social Work (2012) *Professional Capabilities Framework* (PCF) (London: The College of Social Work) www.tcsw.org.uk/pcf.aspx

Warwickshire Safeguarding Adults Partnership (2010) *Serious Case Review. The Murder of Gemma Hayter* (Warwick: Warwickshire Safeguarding Adults Partnership)

Westwood, J (2014) *Children in Need of Support* (Basingstoke: Palgrave Macmillan)

Welsh Institute for Health and Social Care (2010) *Review of In Safe Hands: A Review of the Welsh Assembly Government's Guidance on the Protection of Vulnerable Adults in Wales* (Glamorgan: Welsh Institute for Health and Social Care, University of Glamorgan, Wales)

White, C (2002) 'Re-assessing the social worker's role as an appropriate adult' 24(1) *Journal of Social Welfare and Family Law* 55

Williams, J (2008) 'State responsibility and the abuse of vulnerable older people: is there a case for a public law to protect vulnerable older people from abuse?' in J Bridgeman, H Keating and C Lind (eds), *Responsibility, Law and the Family* (Aldershot: Ashgate)

Williams, J, S Wydall and A Clarke (2013) 'Protecting older victims of abuse who lack capacity: the role of the Independent Mental Capacity Advocate' 3(2) *Elder Law Journal* 167

INDEX